W9-BYF-641

GRAPHIC SCIENCE BIOGRAPHIES

ALBERT EINSTEIN AND THE THEORY OF RELATIVITY

JORDI BAYARRI

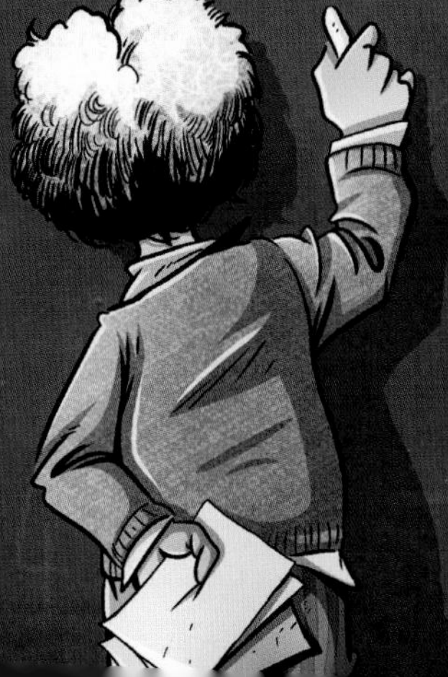

Story and art by Jordi Bayarri
Coloring by Dani Seijas
Historical and scientific consultation by Dr. Tayra M. C. Lanuza-Navarro, PhD in History of Science
Translation by Norwyn MacTíre

First American edition published in 2020 by Graphic Universe™

Graphic Universe™
An imprint of Lerner Publishing Group, Inc.
241 First Avenue North
Minneapolis, MN 55401 USA

For reading levels and more information, look up this title at www.lernerbooks.com.

Image credit: University of New Hampshire/Gado/Getty Images, p. 37

Main body text set in CCDaveGibbonsLower.
Typeface provided by OpenType.

Library of Congress Cataloging-in-Publication Data

Names: Bayarri, Jordi, 1972– author, illustrator.
Title: Albert Einstein and the theory of relativity / Jordi Bayarri.
Description: Minneapolis, MN : Graphic Universe, [2020] I Series: Graphic science biographies I Includes bibliographical references and index. I Audience: 10–14. I Audience: 7 to 8.
Identifiers: LCCN 2019010460 (print) I LCCN 2019016294 (ebook) I ISBN 9781541582378 (eb pdf) I ISBN 9781541578234 (lb ; alk. paper) I ISBN 9781541586963 (pb ; alk. paper)
Subjects: LCSH: Einstein, Albert, 1879–1955—Comic books, strips, etc. I Einstein, Albert, 1879–1955—Juvenile literature. I Physicists—Biography—Comic books, strips, etc. I Physicists—Biography—Juvenile literature.
Classification: LCC QC16.E5 (ebook) I LCC QC16.E5 B38 2020 (print) I DDC 530.092 [B]—dc23

LC record available at https://lccn.loc.gov/2019010460

Manufactured in the United States of America
1-46928-47808-5/2/2019

CONTENTS

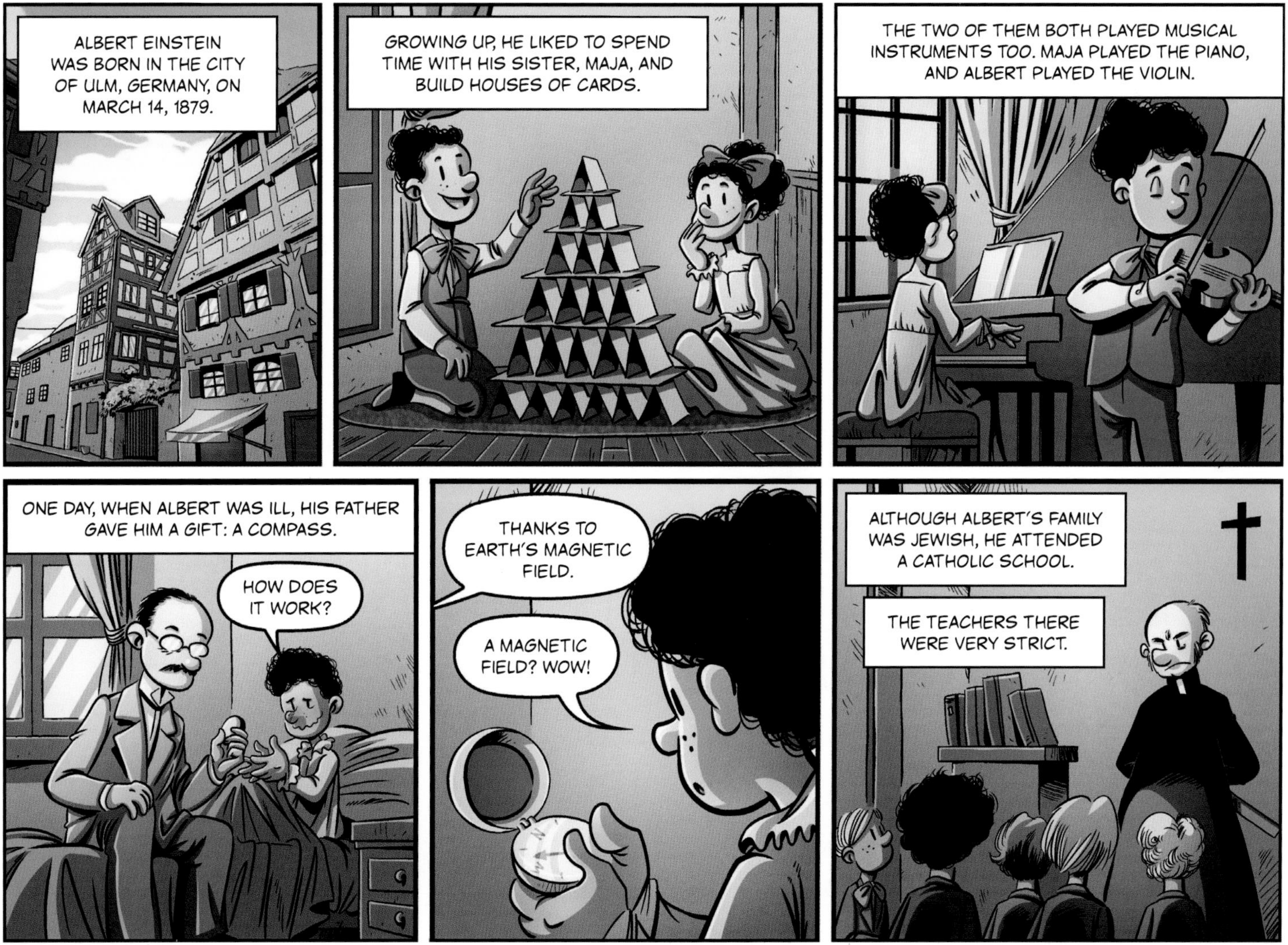
ALBERT EINSTEIN WAS BORN IN THE CITY OF ULM, GERMANY, ON MARCH 14, 1879.
GROWING UP, HE LIKED TO SPEND TIME WITH HIS SISTER, MAJA, AND BUILD HOUSES OF CARDS.
THE TWO OF THEM BOTH PLAYED MUSICAL INSTRUMENTS TOO. MAJA PLAYED THE PIANO, AND ALBERT PLAYED THE VIOLIN.
ONE DAY, WHEN ALBERT WAS ILL, HIS FATHER GAVE HIM A GIFT: A COMPASS.
HOW DOES IT WORK?
THANKS TO EARTH'S MAGNETIC FIELD.
A MAGNETIC FIELD? WOW!
ALTHOUGH ALBERT'S FAMILY WAS JEWISH, HE ATTENDED A CATHOLIC SCHOOL.
THE TEACHERS THERE WERE VERY STRICT.

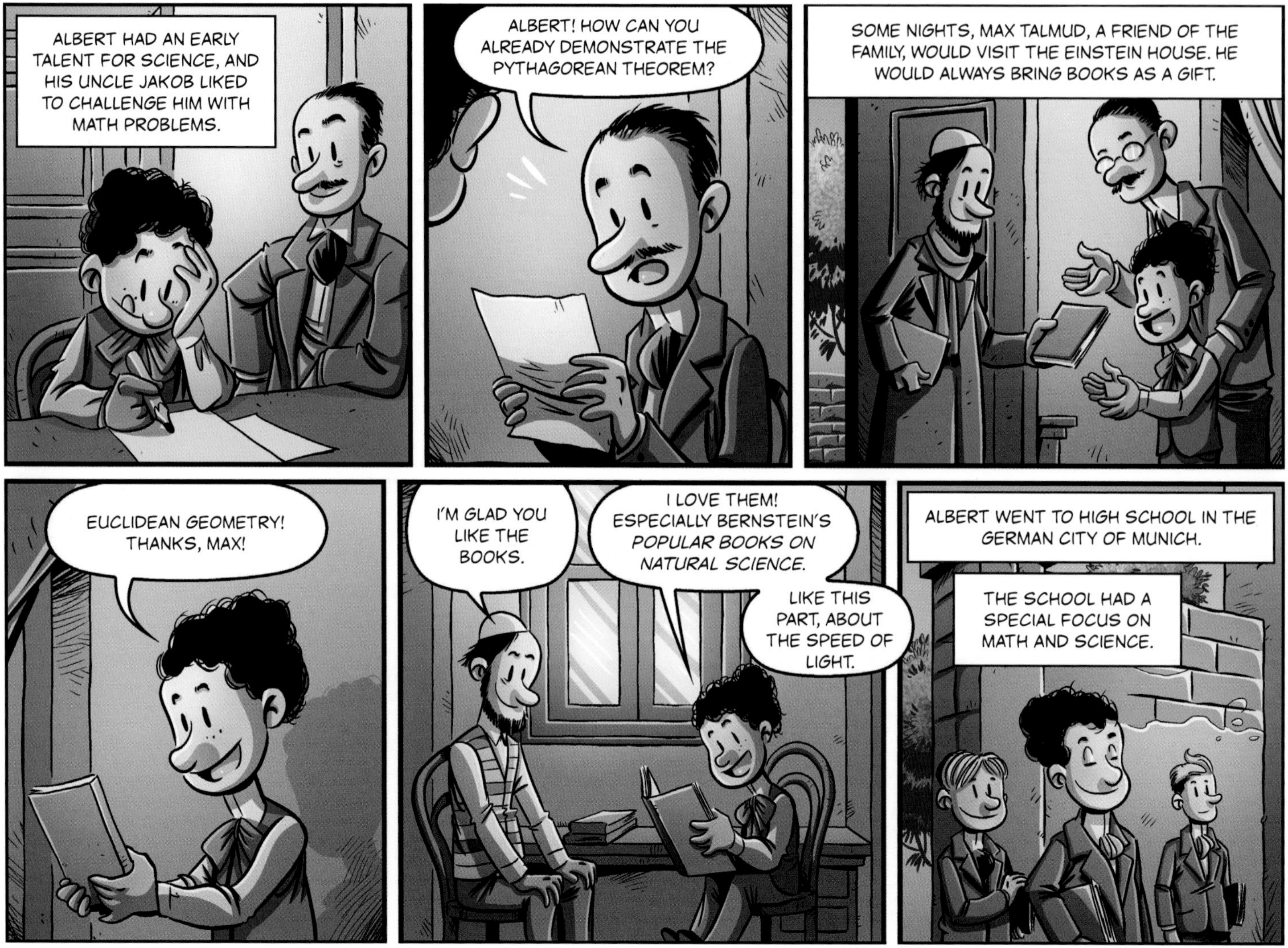
ALBERT HAD AN EARLY TALENT FOR SCIENCE, AND HIS UNCLE JAKOB LIKED TO CHALLENGE HIM WITH MATH PROBLEMS.
ALBERT! HOW CAN YOU ALREADY DEMONSTRATE THE PYTHAGOREAN THEOREM?
SOME NIGHTS, MAX TALMUD, A FRIEND OF THE FAMILY, WOULD VISIT THE EINSTEIN HOUSE. HE WOULD ALWAYS BRING BOOKS AS A GIFT.
EUCLIDEAN GEOMETRY! THANKS, MAX!
I'M GLAD YOU LIKE THE BOOKS.
I LOVE THEM! ESPECIALLY BERNSTEIN'S *POPULAR BOOKS ON NATURAL SCIENCE.*
LIKE THIS PART, ABOUT THE SPEED OF LIGHT.
ALBERT WENT TO HIGH SCHOOL IN THE GERMAN CITY OF MUNICH.
THE SCHOOL HAD A SPECIAL FOCUS ON MATH AND SCIENCE.

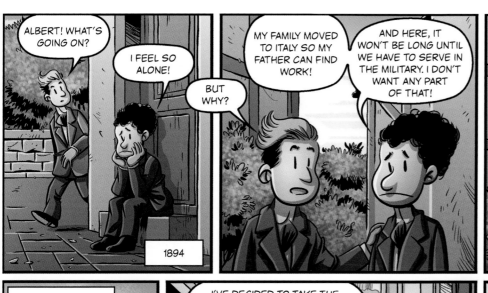

ALBERT! WHAT'S GOING ON?

I FEEL SO ALONE!

BUT WHY?

1894

MY FAMILY MOVED TO ITALY SO MY FATHER CAN FIND WORK!

AND HERE, IT WON'T BE LONG UNTIL WE HAVE TO SERVE IN THE MILITARY. I DON'T WANT ANY PART OF THAT!

I KNOW, BUT . . . WHAT CAN YOU DO?

HMM . . . I HAVE AN IDEA!

A LITTLE LATER, IN PAVIA, ITALY

ALBERT? WHAT ARE YOU DOING HERE?

I'VE DECIDED TO TAKE THE ENTRANCE EXAM FOR THE POLYTECHNIC IN ZÜRICH.

SWITZERLAND!? BUT . . .

THERE'S MORE. RATHER THAN SERVING IN THE MILITARY, I'M GOING TO GIVE UP MY GERMAN CITIZENSHIP.

OH NO!

WHAT IS IT, ALBERT?

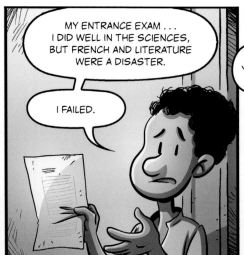

MY ENTRANCE EXAM . . . I DID WELL IN THE SCIENCES, BUT FRENCH AND LITERATURE WERE A DISASTER.

I FAILED.

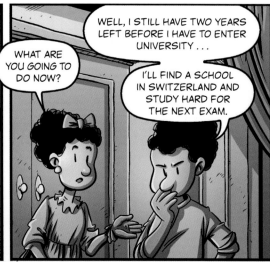

WHAT ARE YOU GOING TO DO NOW?

WELL, I STILL HAVE TWO YEARS LEFT BEFORE I HAVE TO ENTER UNIVERSITY . . .

I'LL FIND A SCHOOL IN SWITZERLAND AND STUDY HARD FOR THE NEXT EXAM.

HELLO, ALBERT. I'M PROFESSOR WINTELER. YOU'LL BE LIVING WITH US WHILE YOU STUDY IN AARAU.

ALFRED WORKED HARD AND KEPT ONE GOAL IN MIND AT ALL TIMES: TO STUDY SCIENCE AND BECOME A PROFESSOR.

I PASSED!

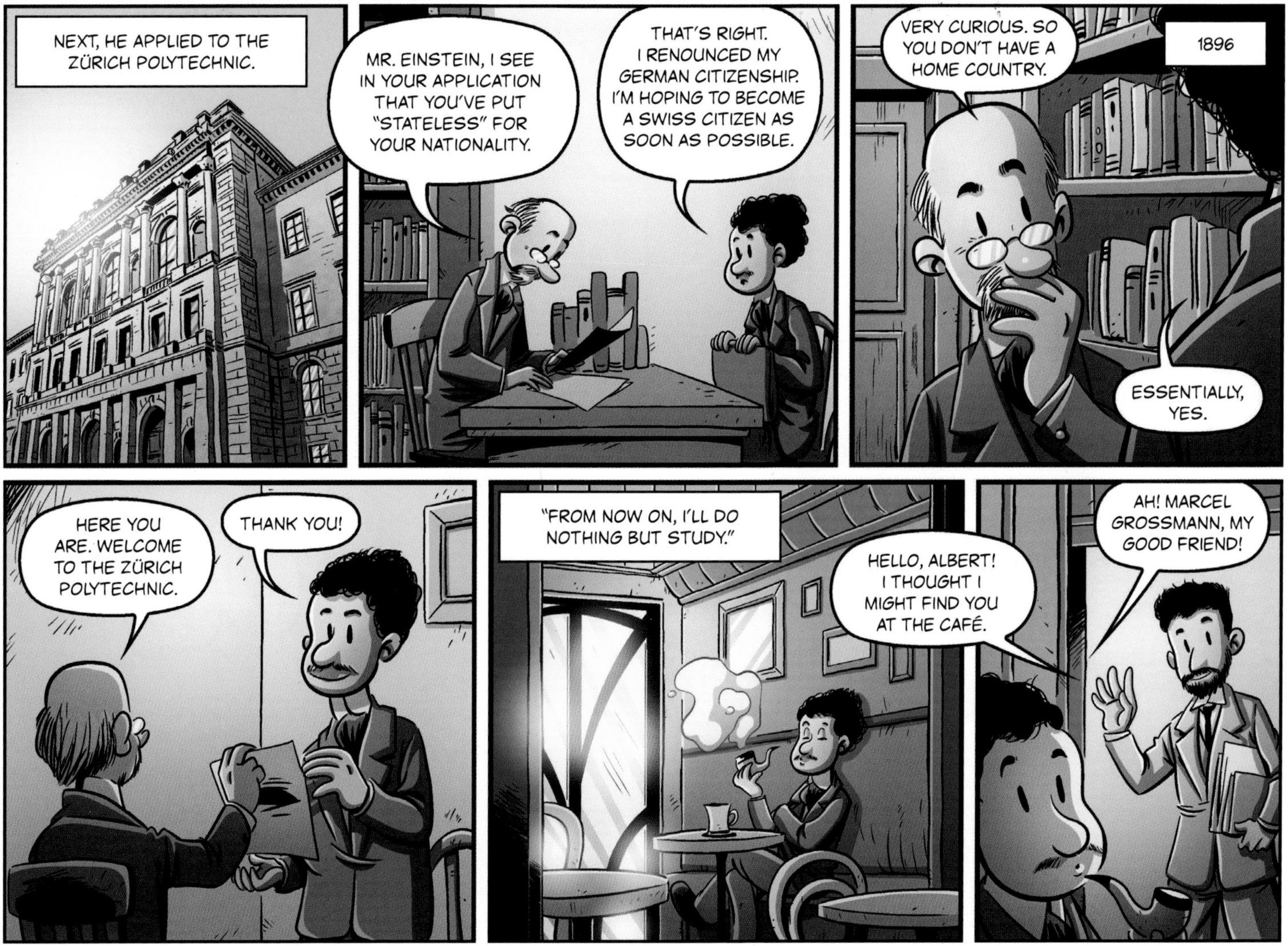
NEXT, HE APPLIED TO THE ZÜRICH POLYTECHNIC.
MR. EINSTEIN, I SEE IN YOUR APPLICATION THAT YOU'VE PUT "STATELESS" FOR YOUR NATIONALITY.
THAT'S RIGHT. I RENOUNCED MY GERMAN CITIZENSHIP. I'M HOPING TO BECOME A SWISS CITIZEN AS SOON AS POSSIBLE.
1896
VERY CURIOUS. SO YOU DON'T HAVE A HOME COUNTRY.
ESSENTIALLY, YES.
HERE YOU ARE. WELCOME TO THE ZÜRICH POLYTECHNIC.
THANK YOU!
"FROM NOW ON, I'LL DO NOTHING BUT STUDY."
HELLO, ALBERT! I THOUGHT I MIGHT FIND YOU AT THE CAFÉ.
AH! MARCEL GROSSMANN, MY GOOD FRIEND!

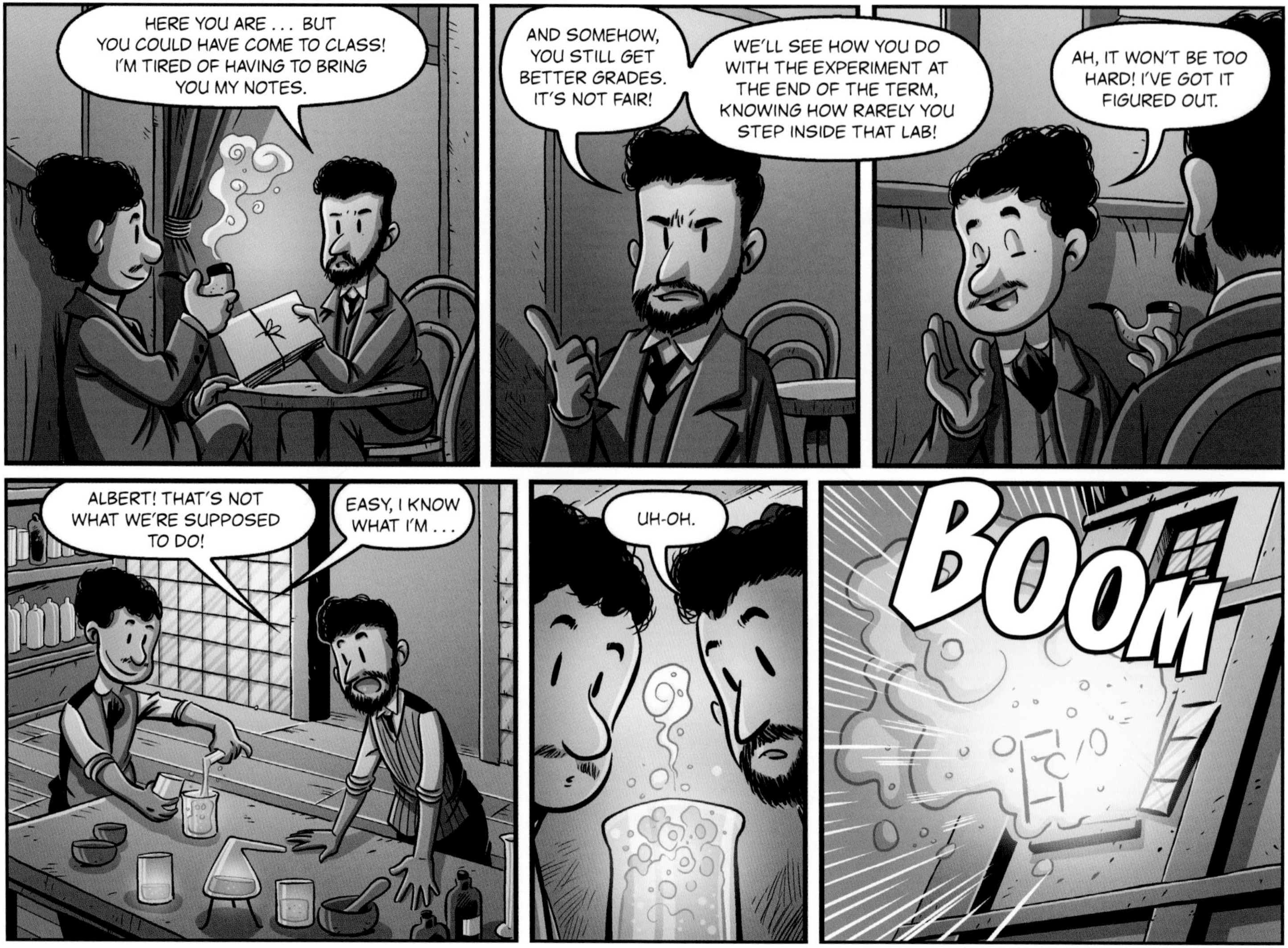
HERE YOU ARE . . . BUT YOU COULD HAVE COME TO CLASS! I'M TIRED OF HAVING TO BRING YOU MY NOTES.
AND SOMEHOW, YOU STILL GET BETTER GRADES. IT'S NOT FAIR!
WE'LL SEE HOW YOU DO WITH THE EXPERIMENT AT THE END OF THE TERM, KNOWING HOW RARELY YOU STEP INSIDE THAT LAB!
AH, IT WON'T BE TOO HARD! I'VE GOT IT FIGURED OUT.
ALBERT! THAT'S NOT WHAT WE'RE SUPPOSED TO DO!
EASY, I KNOW WHAT I'M . . .
UH-OH.
BOOM

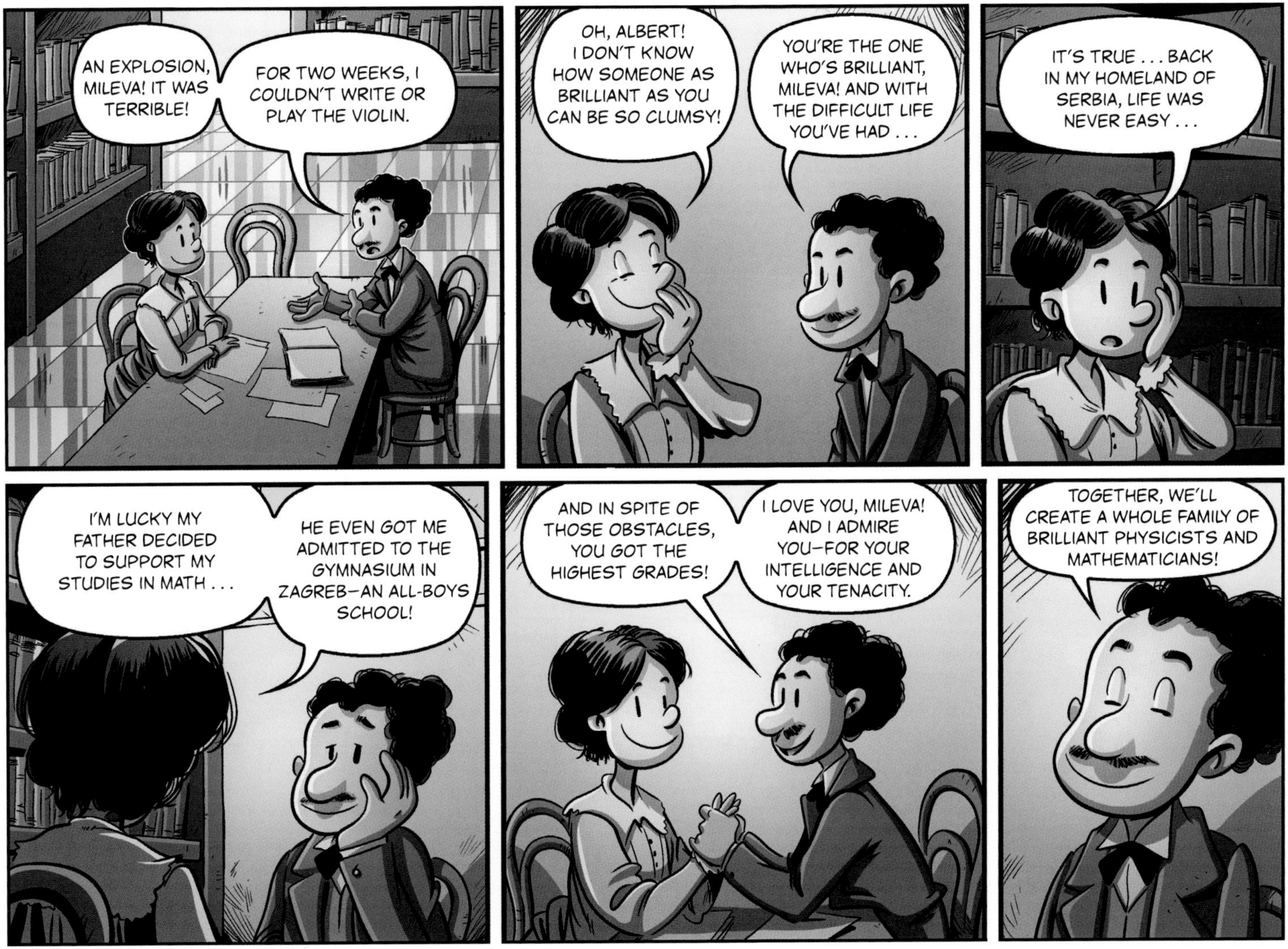
AN EXPLOSION, MILEVA! IT WAS TERRIBLE!
FOR TWO WEEKS, I COULDN'T WRITE OR PLAY THE VIOLIN.
OH, ALBERT! I DON'T KNOW HOW SOMEONE AS BRILLIANT AS YOU CAN BE SO CLUMSY!
YOU'RE THE ONE WHO'S BRILLIANT, MILEVA! AND WITH THE DIFFICULT LIFE YOU'VE HAD . . .
IT'S TRUE . . . BACK IN MY HOMELAND OF SERBIA, LIFE WAS NEVER EASY . . .
I'M LUCKY MY FATHER DECIDED TO SUPPORT MY STUDIES IN MATH . . .
HE EVEN GOT ME ADMITTED TO THE GYMNASIUM IN ZAGREB—AN ALL-BOYS SCHOOL!
AND IN SPITE OF THOSE OBSTACLES, YOU GOT THE HIGHEST GRADES!
I LOVE YOU, MILEVA! AND I ADMIRE YOU—FOR YOUR INTELLIGENCE AND YOUR TENACITY.
TOGETHER, WE'LL CREATE A WHOLE FAMILY OF BRILLIANT PHYSICISTS AND MATHEMATICIANS!

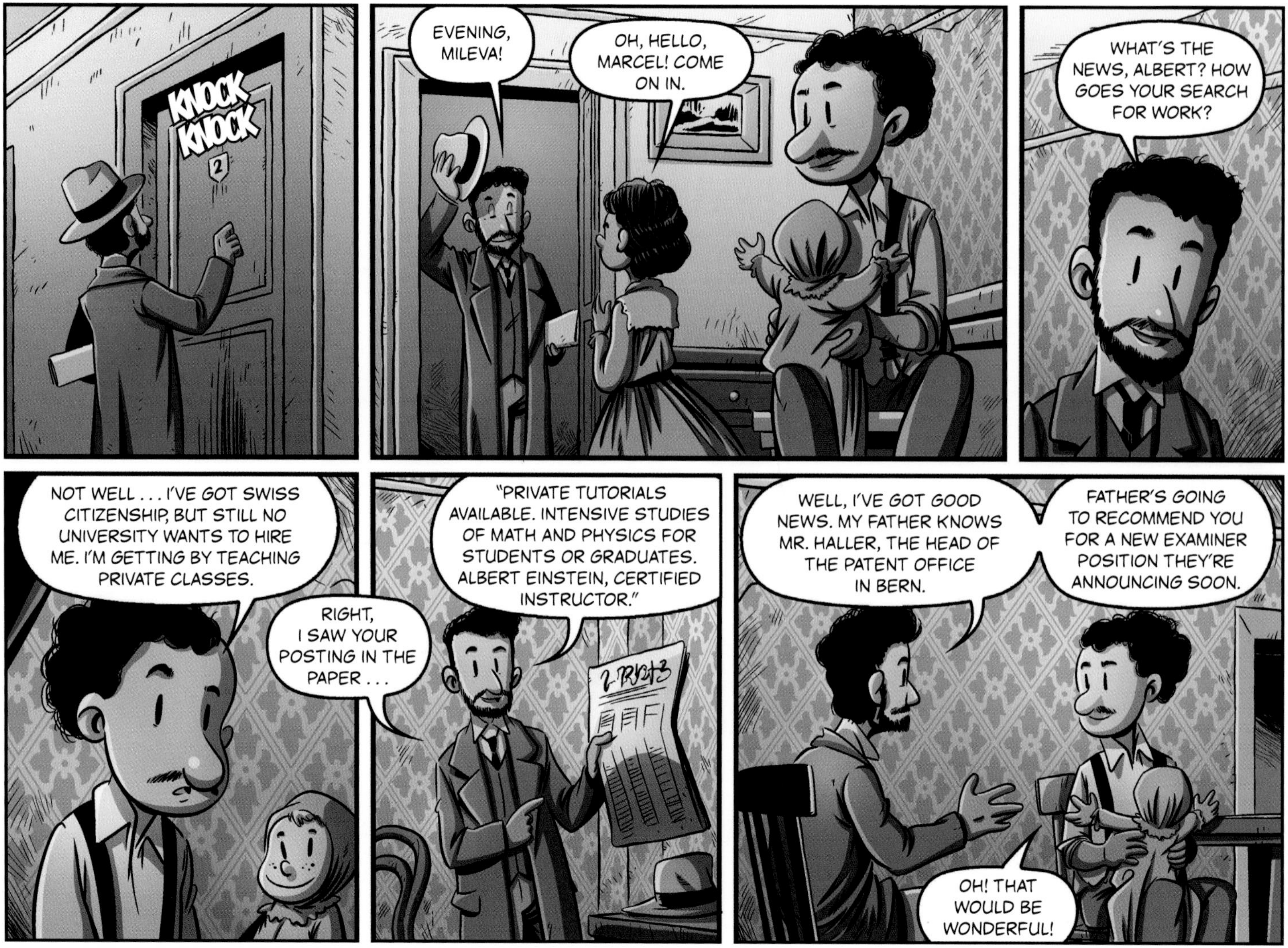
KNOCK KNOCK
2
EVENING, MILEVA!
OH, HELLO, MARCEL! COME ON IN.
WHAT'S THE NEWS, ALBERT? HOW GOES YOUR SEARCH FOR WORK?
NOT WELL . . . I'VE GOT SWISS CITIZENSHIP, BUT STILL NO UNIVERSITY WANTS TO HIRE ME. I'M GETTING BY TEACHING PRIVATE CLASSES.
RIGHT, I SAW YOUR POSTING IN THE PAPER . . .
"PRIVATE TUTORIALS AVAILABLE. INTENSIVE STUDIES OF MATH AND PHYSICS FOR STUDENTS OR GRADUATES. ALBERT EINSTEIN, CERTIFIED INSTRUCTOR."
WELL, I'VE GOT GOOD NEWS. MY FATHER KNOWS MR. HALLER, THE HEAD OF THE PATENT OFFICE IN BERN.
FATHER'S GOING TO RECOMMEND YOU FOR A NEW EXAMINER POSITION THEY'RE ANNOUNCING SOON.
OH! THAT WOULD BE WONDERFUL!

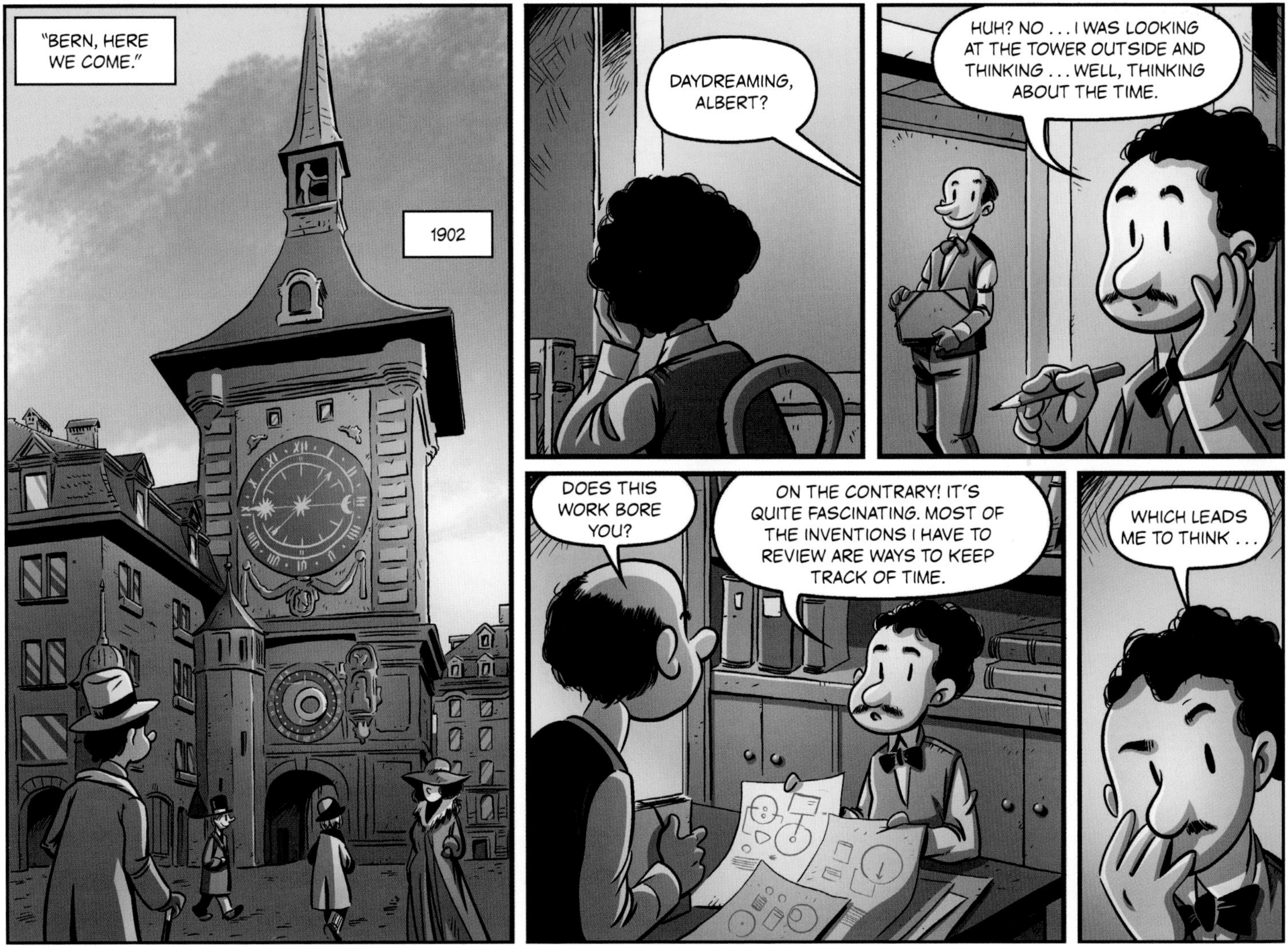
"BERN, HERE WE COME."
1902
DAYDREAMING, ALBERT?
HUH? NO . . . I WAS LOOKING AT THE TOWER OUTSIDE AND THINKING . . . WELL, THINKING ABOUT THE TIME.
DOES THIS WORK BORE YOU?
ON THE CONTRARY! IT'S QUITE FASCINATING. MOST OF THE INVENTIONS I HAVE TO REVIEW ARE WAYS TO KEEP TRACK OF TIME.
WHICH LEADS ME TO THINK . . .

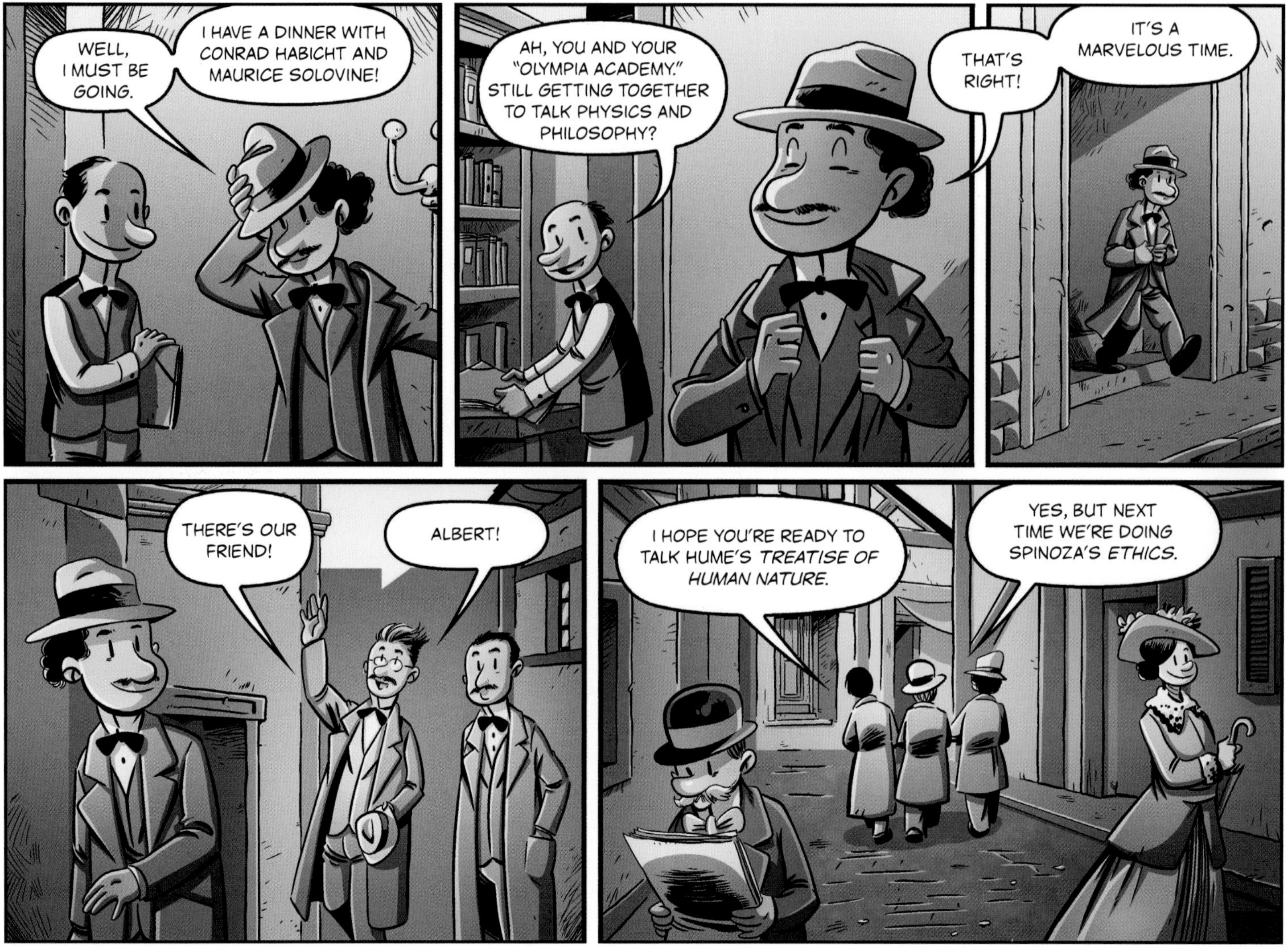
WELL, I MUST BE GOING.
I HAVE A DINNER WITH CONRAD HABICHT AND MAURICE SOLOVINE!
AH, YOU AND YOUR "OLYMPIA ACADEMY." STILL GETTING TOGETHER TO TALK PHYSICS AND PHILOSOPHY?
THAT'S RIGHT!
IT'S A MARVELOUS TIME.
THERE'S OUR FRIEND!
ALBERT!
I HOPE YOU'RE READY TO TALK HUME'S *TREATISE OF HUMAN NATURE.*
YES, BUT NEXT TIME WE'RE DOING SPINOZA'S *ETHICS.*

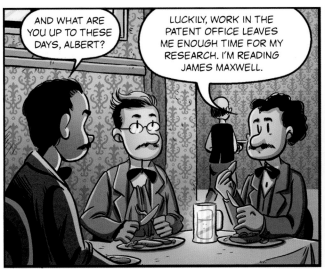

AND WHAT ARE YOU UP TO THESE DAYS, ALBERT?

LUCKILY, WORK IN THE PATENT OFFICE LEAVES ME ENOUGH TIME FOR MY RESEARCH. I'M READING JAMES MAXWELL.

HIS EQUATIONS SEEK TO PROVE WHAT FARADAY SAID ABOUT MAGNETIC FIELDS. IT'S VERY INTERESTING. ALTHOUGH THEY AREN'T COMPATIBLE WITH CLASSICAL MECHANICS!

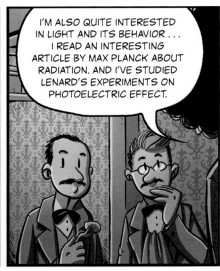

I'M ALSO QUITE INTERESTED IN LIGHT AND ITS BEHAVIOR . . . I READ AN INTERESTING ARTICLE BY MAX PLANCK ABOUT RADIATION. AND I'VE STUDIED LENARD'S EXPERIMENTS ON PHOTOELECTRIC EFFECT.

I'VE REACHED THE CONCLUSION THAT LIGHT IS NOT A CONTINUOUS WAVE. RATHER, IT'S COMPOSED OF SMALL PARTICLES. PLANCK CALLED THEM QUANTA.

BUT . . . DID YOU DO ANY EXPERIMENTS ON THIS?

OH, NO.

THESE ARE JUST MY THOUGHTS. BUT I'M CONSTANTLY DOING MENTAL EXPERIMENTS TO TEST MY THEORIES.

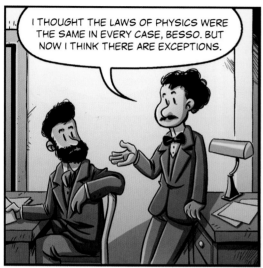

I THOUGHT THE LAWS OF PHYSICS WERE THE SAME IN EVERY CASE, BESSO. BUT NOW I THINK THERE ARE EXCEPTIONS.

FOR EXAMPLE, DO THE CLASSICAL LAWS OF PHYSICS STAY THE SAME AT THE SPEED OF LIGHT?

"IT'S SOMETHING I'VE WONDERED SINCE I WAS SIXTEEN YEARS OLD..."

"...WHEN I IMAGINED WHAT IT WOULD BE LIKE TO TRAVEL ON A RAY OF LIGHT."

AND WHAT HAVE YOU CONCLUDED?

THAT FOR AN OBSERVER MOVING AT A CERTAIN SPEED, TIME DOESN'T PASS IN THE SAME WAY AS IT DOES FOR SOMEONE *OUTSIDE* OF THE SYSTEM IN MOTION.

EACH FRAME OF REFERENCE HAS ITS OWN RELATIVE TIME.

IT DEPENDS ON HOW FAST *WE'RE* MOVING AND HOW FAST THE *OBJECT WE'RE MEASURING* IS MOVING.

AND SO CLASSICAL PHYSICS FAILS US IN THESE CASES.

TIME IS NOT AN ABSOLUTE THING.

MARCEL, THIS ARTICLE ABOUT MY THEORY OF INVARIANCE HAS LEFT ME EXHAUSTED!

I CAN TELL.

1905

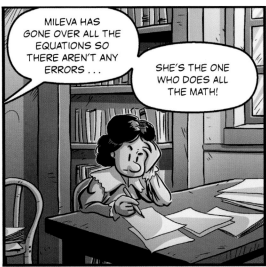

MILEVA HAS GONE OVER ALL THE EQUATIONS SO THERE AREN'T ANY ERRORS . . .

SHE'S THE ONE WHO DOES ALL THE MATH!

AND I BET YOU'RE ALREADY THINKING ABOUT YOUR *NEXT* ARTICLE, RIGHT?

YES, OF COURSE . . . IN THE NEXT ONE, I'LL EXPLAIN MY THEORY THAT MASS AND ENERGY ARE THE SAME.

I STILL HAVE TO REREAD IT . . . BUT I'VE BOILED EVERYTHING DOWN TO A SINGLE EQUATION.

LET'S SEE.

AMAZING!

$$E = MC^2$$

MAX PLANCK HAS INCLUDED YOUR THEORY OF SPECIAL RELATIVITY IN HIS LATEST ARTICLE. YOU'LL BE HAPPY NOW, RIGHT?

INDEED! PLANCK IS A GREAT MATHEMATICIAN AND PHYSICIST. IT'S A TRUE HONOR!

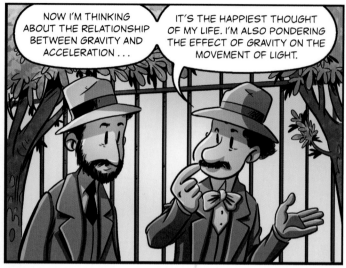

NOW I'M THINKING ABOUT THE RELATIONSHIP BETWEEN GRAVITY AND ACCELERATION . . .

IT'S THE HAPPIEST THOUGHT OF MY LIFE. I'M ALSO PONDERING THE EFFECT OF GRAVITY ON THE MOVEMENT OF LIGHT.

THAT IS . . . IF LIGHT IS MADE OUT OF QUANTA, OUT OF PARTICLES, IT HAS TO BE AFFECTED BY GRAVITY.

BUT THE SPEED OF LIGHT IS ALWAYS THE SAME. THE FRAME OF REFERENCE DOESN'T MATTER! EVEN AT AN ATOMIC SCALE!

SOON I'LL ATTEND THE FIRST SOLVAY CONFERENCE, IN BELGIUM.

THE MOST BRILLIANT PHYSICISTS IN EUROPE ARE GOING TO MEET. THERE, I CAN TALK ABOUT ALL THIS AND SHARE MY DOUBTS.

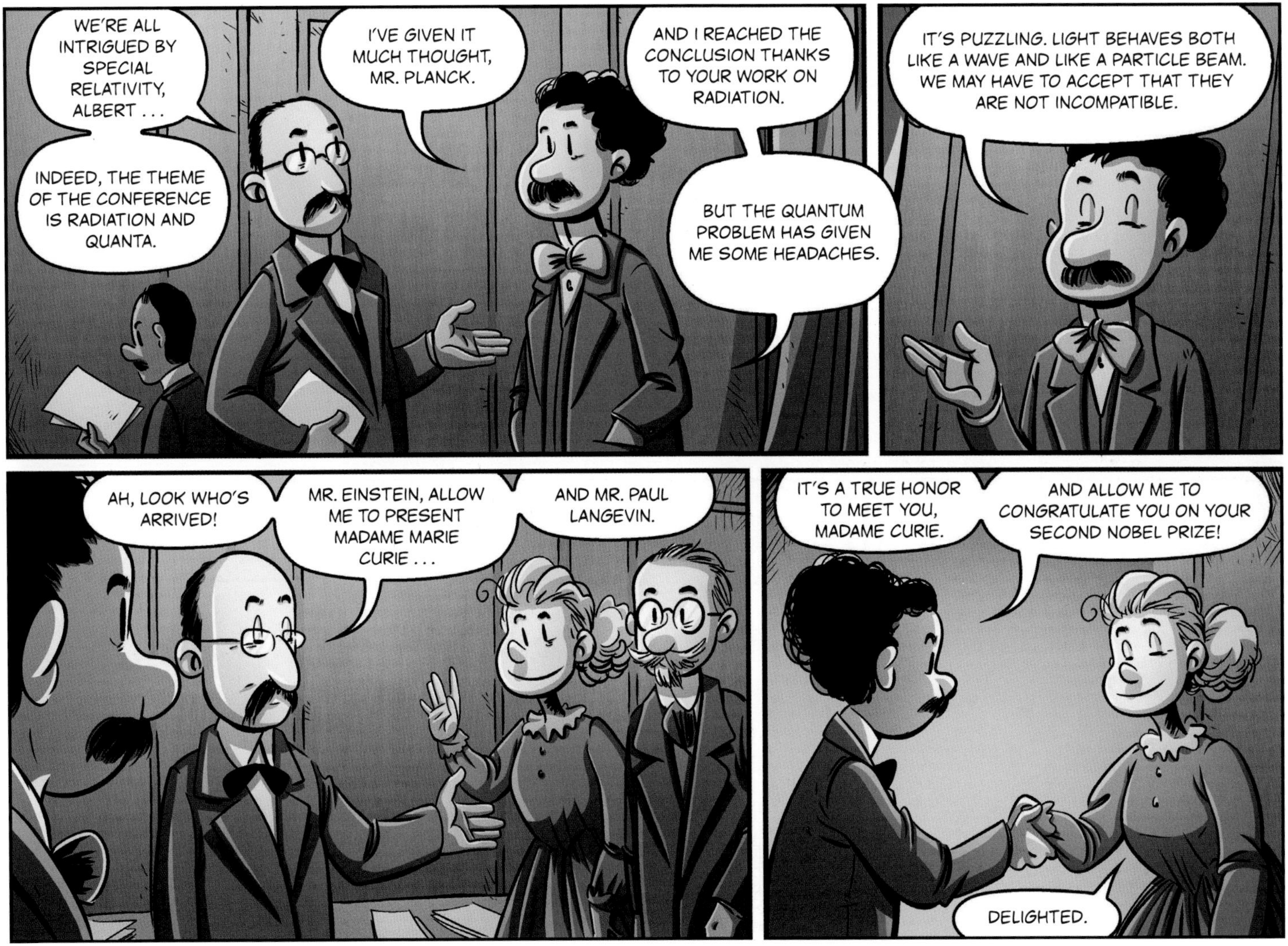
WE'RE ALL INTRIGUED BY SPECIAL RELATIVITY, ALBERT . . .
INDEED, THE THEME OF THE CONFERENCE IS RADIATION AND QUANTA.
I'VE GIVEN IT MUCH THOUGHT, MR. PLANCK.
AND I REACHED THE CONCLUSION THANKS TO YOUR WORK ON RADIATION.
BUT THE QUANTUM PROBLEM HAS GIVEN ME SOME HEADACHES.
IT'S PUZZLING. LIGHT BEHAVES BOTH LIKE A WAVE AND LIKE A PARTICLE BEAM. WE MAY HAVE TO ACCEPT THAT THEY ARE NOT INCOMPATIBLE.
AH, LOOK WHO'S ARRIVED!
MR. EINSTEIN, ALLOW ME TO PRESENT MADAME MARIE CURIE . . .
AND MR. PAUL LANGEVIN.
IT'S A TRUE HONOR TO MEET YOU, MADAME CURIE.
AND ALLOW ME TO CONGRATULATE YOU ON YOUR SECOND NOBEL PRIZE!
DELIGHTED.

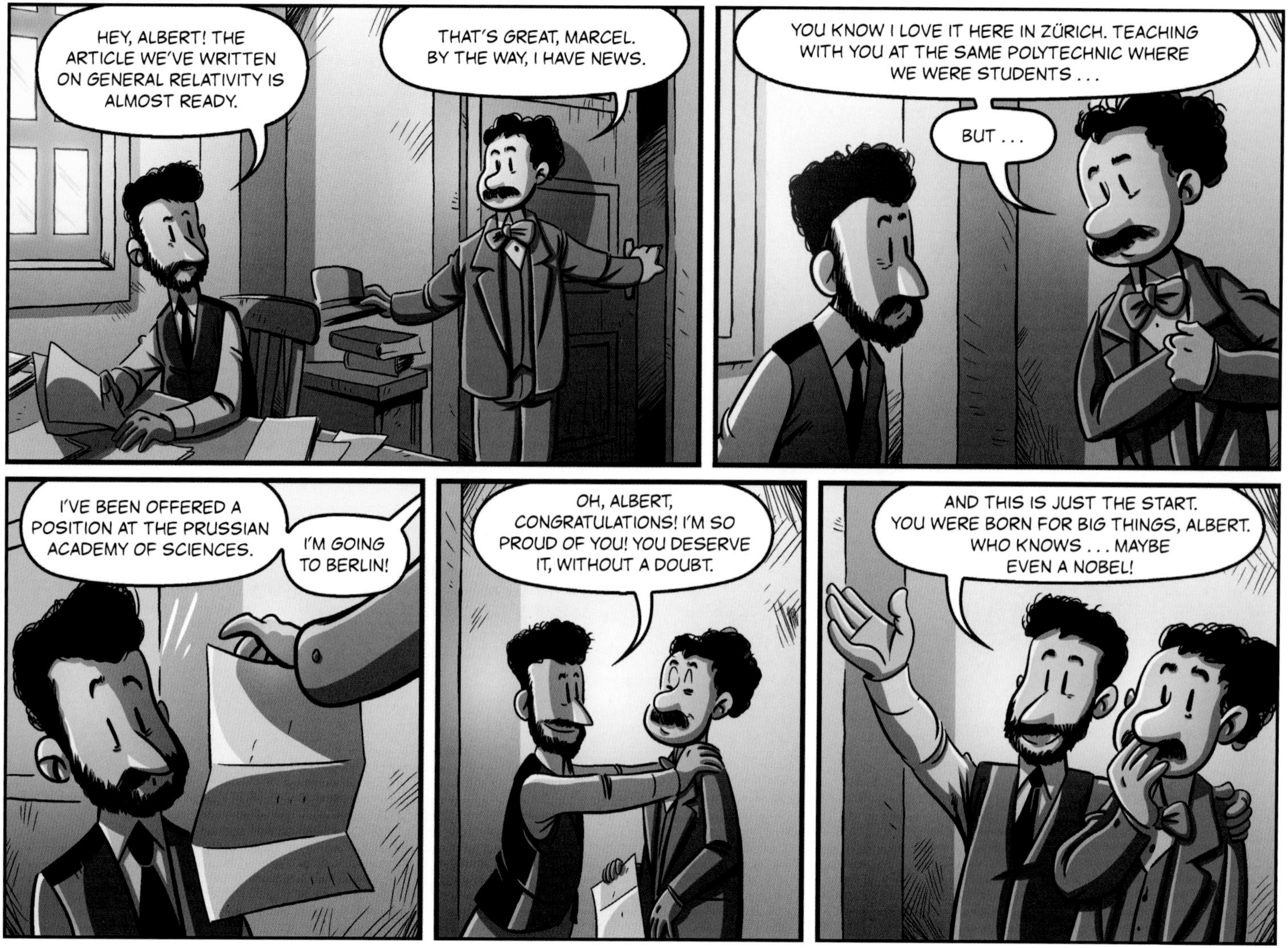
HEY, ALBERT! THE ARTICLE WE'VE WRITTEN ON GENERAL RELATIVITY IS ALMOST READY.
THAT'S GREAT, MARCEL. BY THE WAY, I HAVE NEWS.
YOU KNOW I LOVE IT HERE IN ZÜRICH. TEACHING WITH YOU AT THE SAME POLYTECHNIC WHERE WE WERE STUDENTS . . .
BUT . . .
I'VE BEEN OFFERED A POSITION AT THE PRUSSIAN ACADEMY OF SCIENCES.
I'M GOING TO BERLIN!
OH, ALBERT, CONGRATULATIONS! I'M SO PROUD OF YOU! YOU DESERVE IT, WITHOUT A DOUBT.
AND THIS IS JUST THE START. YOU WERE BORN FOR BIG THINGS, ALBERT. WHO KNOWS . . . MAYBE EVEN A NOBEL!

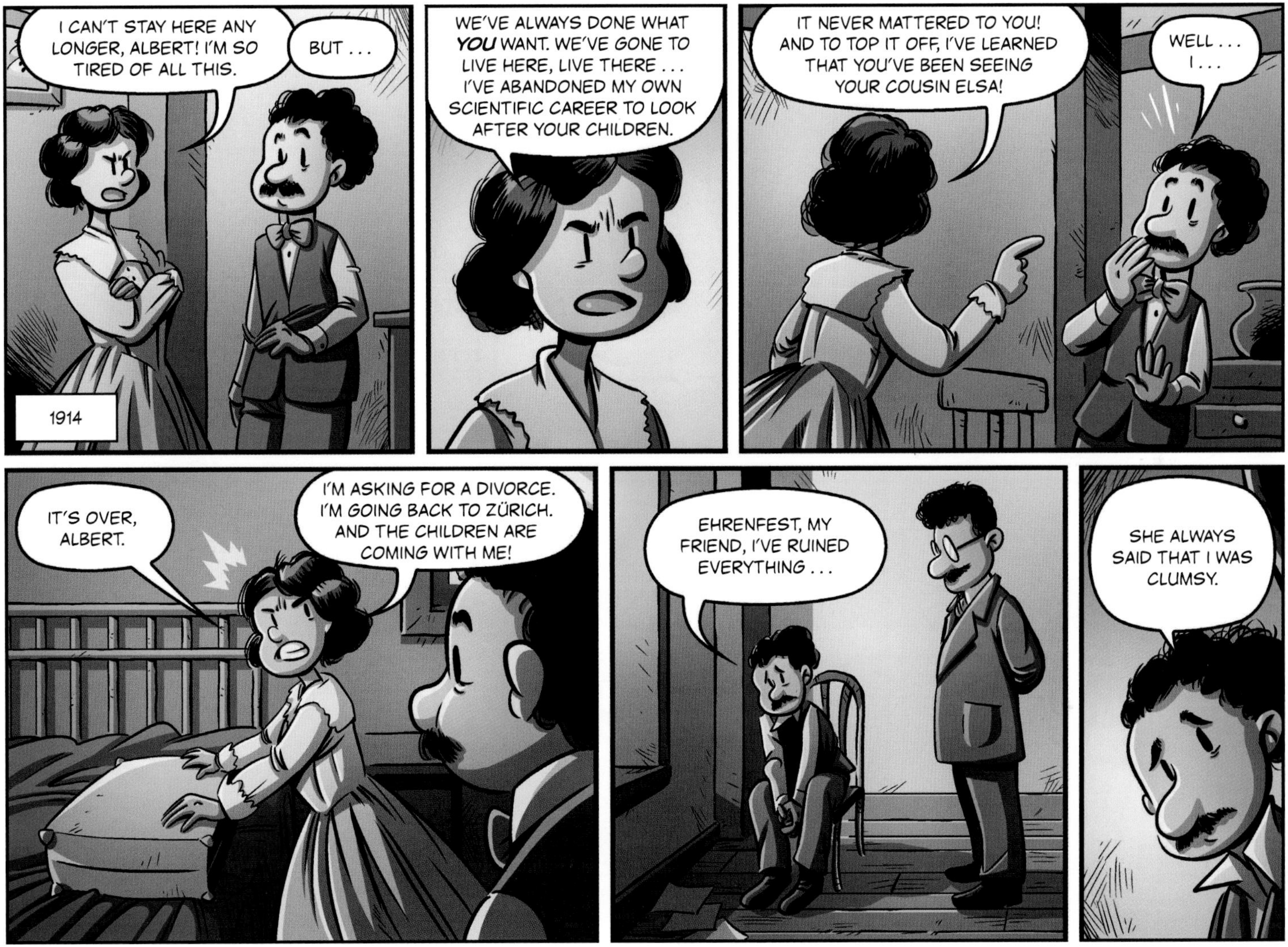
I CAN'T STAY HERE ANY LONGER, ALBERT! I'M SO TIRED OF ALL THIS.
BUT . . .
1914
WE'VE ALWAYS DONE WHAT ***YOU*** WANT. WE'VE GONE TO LIVE HERE, LIVE THERE . . . I'VE ABANDONED MY OWN SCIENTIFIC CAREER TO LOOK AFTER YOUR CHILDREN.
IT NEVER MATTERED TO YOU! AND TO TOP IT OFF, I'VE LEARNED THAT YOU'VE BEEN SEEING YOUR COUSIN ELSA!
WELL . . . I . . .
IT'S OVER, ALBERT.
I'M ASKING FOR A DIVORCE. I'M GOING BACK TO ZÜRICH. AND THE CHILDREN ARE COMING WITH ME!
EHRENFEST, MY FRIEND, I'VE RUINED EVERYTHING . . .
SHE ALWAYS SAID THAT I WAS CLUMSY.

OH **NO!** HOW AWFUL!

WHAT HAPPENED? BAD NEWS?

PAUL, DO YOU REMEMBER WHAT I SAID ABOUT NEEDING CERTAIN MEASUREMENTS TO VERIFY MY THEORY OF RELATIVITY?

THE IDEA WAS TO TAKE ADVANTAGE OF AN UPCOMING ECLIPSE. WE'D SEE HOW THE GRAVITATIONAL FIELD OF THE SUN AFFECTS THE RAYS OF LIGHT. AND IT WOULD CONFIRM THAT LIGHT IS CURVED BECAUSE OF GRAVITY.

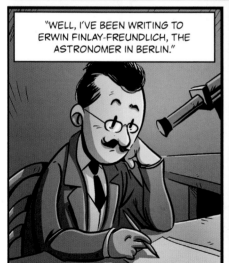

"WELL, I'VE BEEN WRITING TO ERWIN FINLAY-FREUNDLICH, THE ASTRONOMER IN BERLIN."

WE STARTED RAISING FUNDS TO FINANCE AN EXPEDITION. I EVEN OFFERED TO PROVIDE THE MONEY IF WE DIDN'T GET ENOUGH!

"FINALLY, THE EXPEDITION LEFT FOR THE CRIMEAN PENINSULA, NEAR RUSSIA. IT'S THE BEST PLACE TO TAKE OUR MEASUREMENTS."

"BUT THE WAR HAD JUST BROKEN OUT. THE RUSSIANS TOOK THEM FOR SPIES."

"THEY'VE IMPRISONED OUR MEN!"

THIS WAR! IT'S HORRIBLE!

THE BORDERS ARE CLOSED. I CAN'T EVEN GO TO ZÜRICH TO SEE MY CHILDREN.

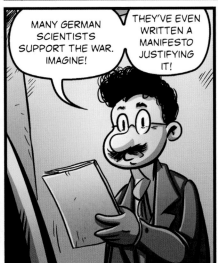

MANY GERMAN SCIENTISTS SUPPORT THE WAR. IMAGINE!

THEY'VE EVEN WRITTEN A MANIFESTO JUSTIFYING IT!

I KNOW, AND SOME HAVE EVEN LENT THEIR KNOWLEDGE TO THE WAR EFFORT . . . MAKING THE DEATH GAS THEY'RE USING IN THE TRENCHES.

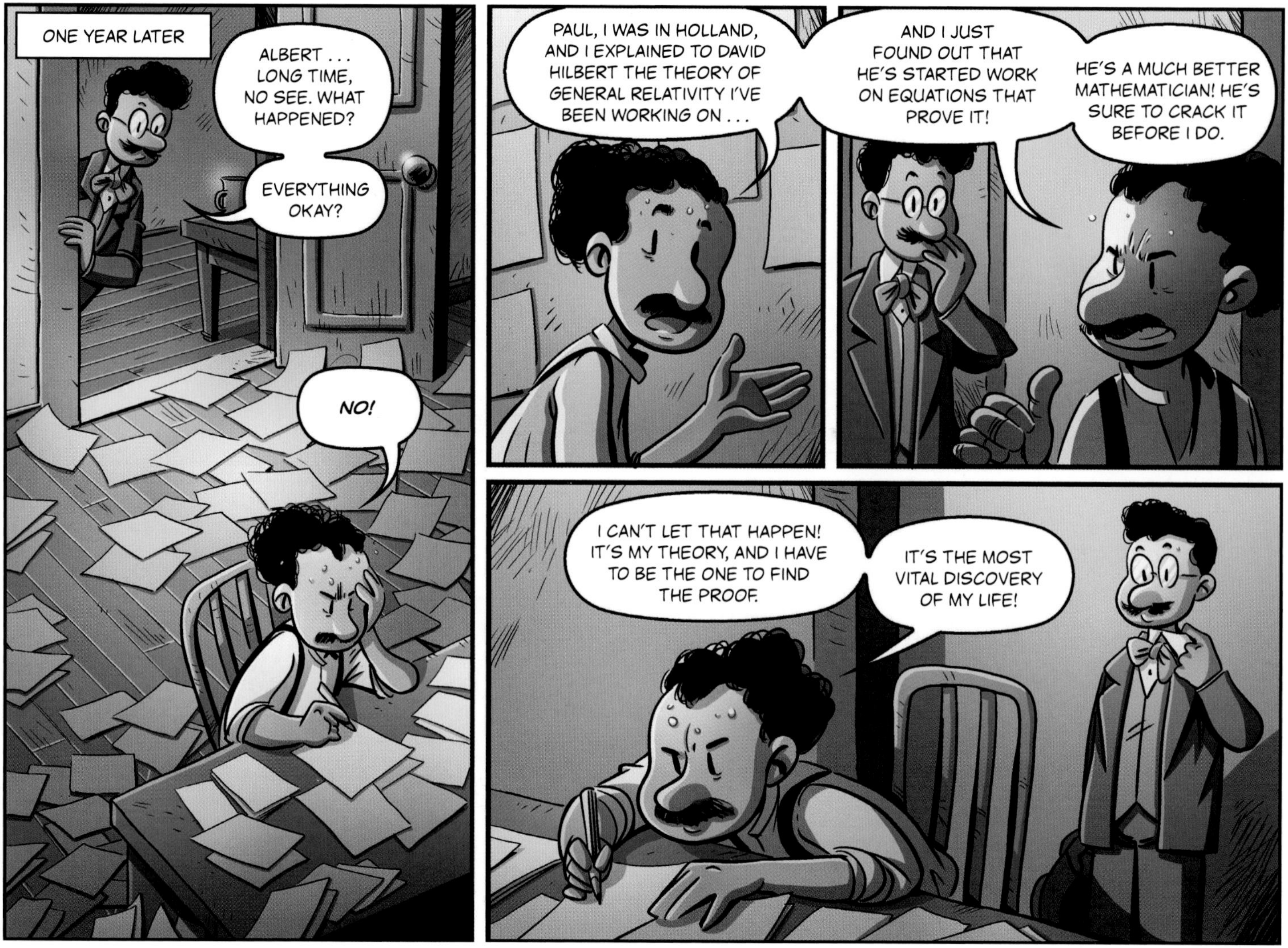
ONE YEAR LATER
ALBERT . . . LONG TIME, NO SEE. WHAT HAPPENED?
EVERYTHING OKAY?
NO!
PAUL, I WAS IN HOLLAND, AND I EXPLAINED TO DAVID HILBERT THE THEORY OF GENERAL RELATIVITY I'VE BEEN WORKING ON . . .
AND I JUST FOUND OUT THAT HE'S STARTED WORK ON EQUATIONS THAT PROVE IT!
HE'S A MUCH BETTER MATHEMATICIAN! HE'S SURE TO CRACK IT BEFORE I DO.
I CAN'T LET THAT HAPPEN! IT'S MY THEORY, AND I HAVE TO BE THE ONE TO FIND THE PROOF.
IT'S THE MOST VITAL DISCOVERY OF MY LIFE!

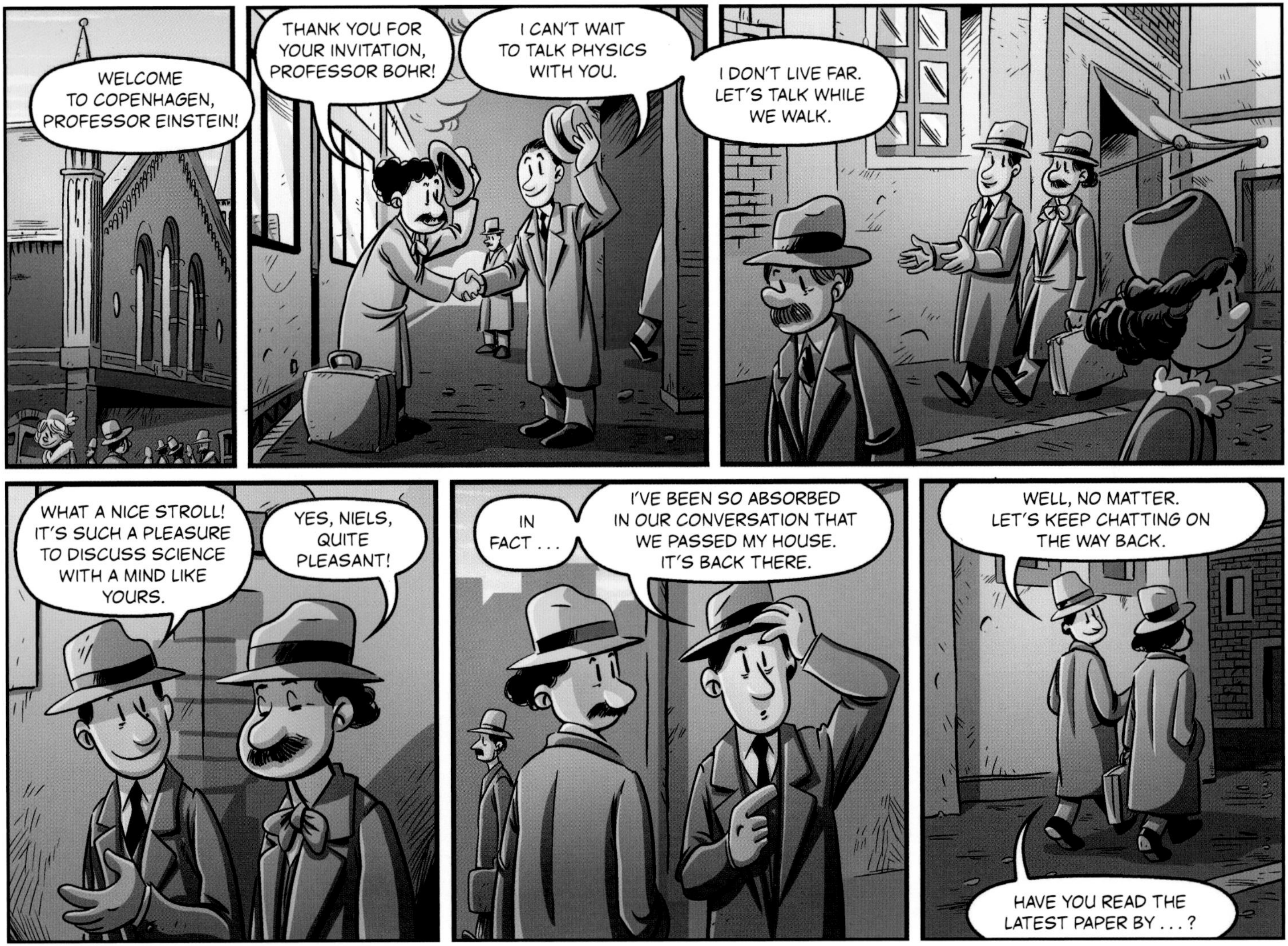
WELCOME TO COPENHAGEN, PROFESSOR EINSTEIN!
THANK YOU FOR YOUR INVITATION, PROFESSOR BOHR!
I CAN'T WAIT TO TALK PHYSICS WITH YOU.
I DON'T LIVE FAR. LET'S TALK WHILE WE WALK.
WHAT A NICE STROLL! IT'S SUCH A PLEASURE TO DISCUSS SCIENCE WITH A MIND LIKE YOURS.
YES, NIELS, QUITE PLEASANT!
IN FACT . . .
I'VE BEEN SO ABSORBED IN OUR CONVERSATION THAT WE PASSED MY HOUSE. IT'S BACK THERE.
WELL, NO MATTER. LET'S KEEP CHATTING ON THE WAY BACK.
HAVE YOU READ THE LATEST PAPER BY . . . ?

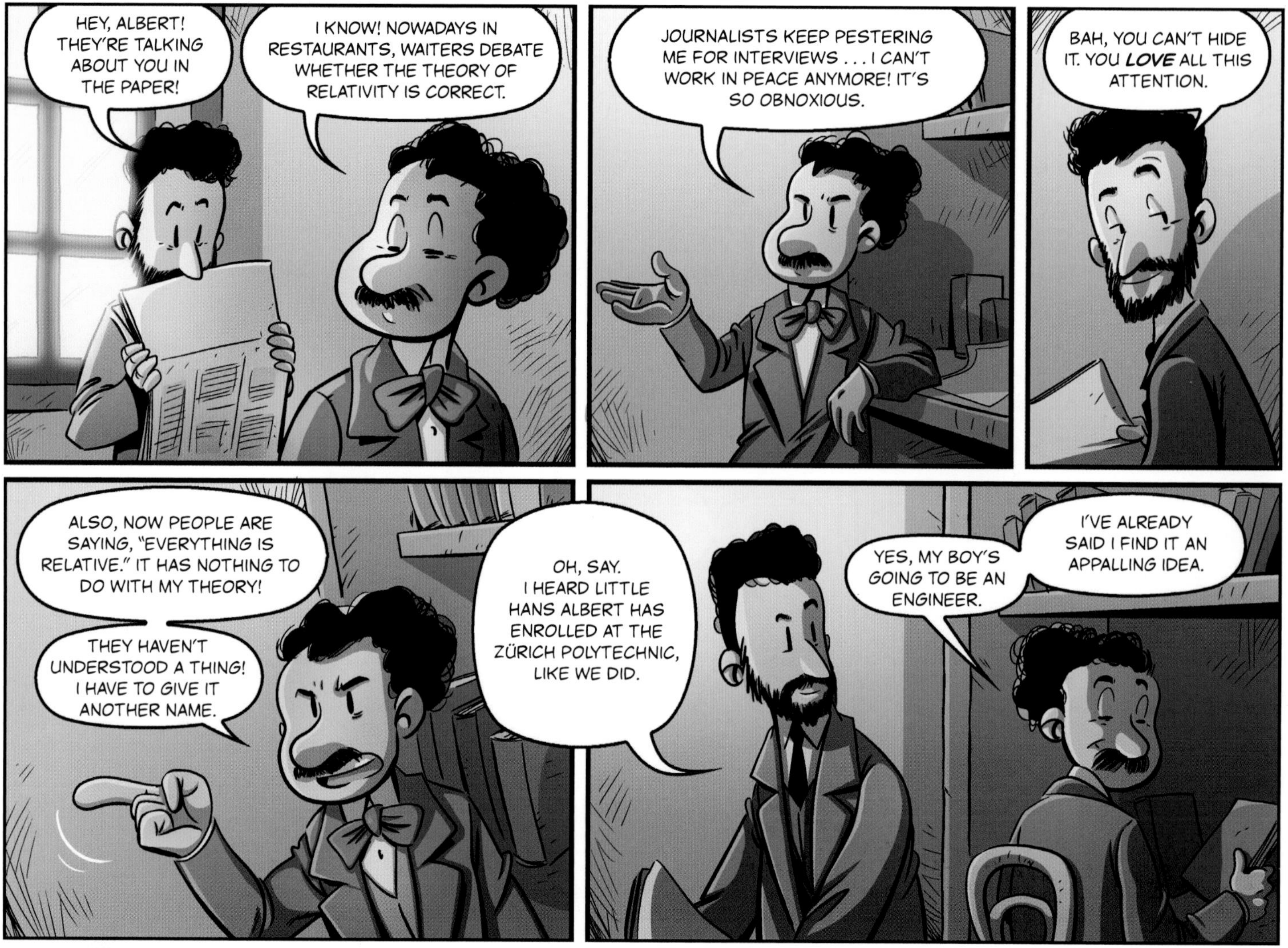
HEY, ALBERT! THEY'RE TALKING ABOUT YOU IN THE PAPER!
I KNOW! NOWADAYS IN RESTAURANTS, WAITERS DEBATE WHETHER THE THEORY OF RELATIVITY IS CORRECT.
JOURNALISTS KEEP PESTERING ME FOR INTERVIEWS . . . I CAN'T WORK IN PEACE ANYMORE! IT'S SO OBNOXIOUS.
BAH, YOU CAN'T HIDE IT. YOU **LOVE** ALL THIS ATTENTION.
ALSO, NOW PEOPLE ARE SAYING, "EVERYTHING IS RELATIVE." IT HAS NOTHING TO DO WITH MY THEORY!
THEY HAVEN'T UNDERSTOOD A THING! I HAVE TO GIVE IT ANOTHER NAME.
OH, SAY. I HEARD LITTLE HANS ALBERT HAS ENROLLED AT THE ZÜRICH POLYTECHNIC, LIKE WE DID.
YES, MY BOY'S GOING TO BE AN ENGINEER.
I'VE ALREADY SAID I FIND IT AN APPALLING IDEA.

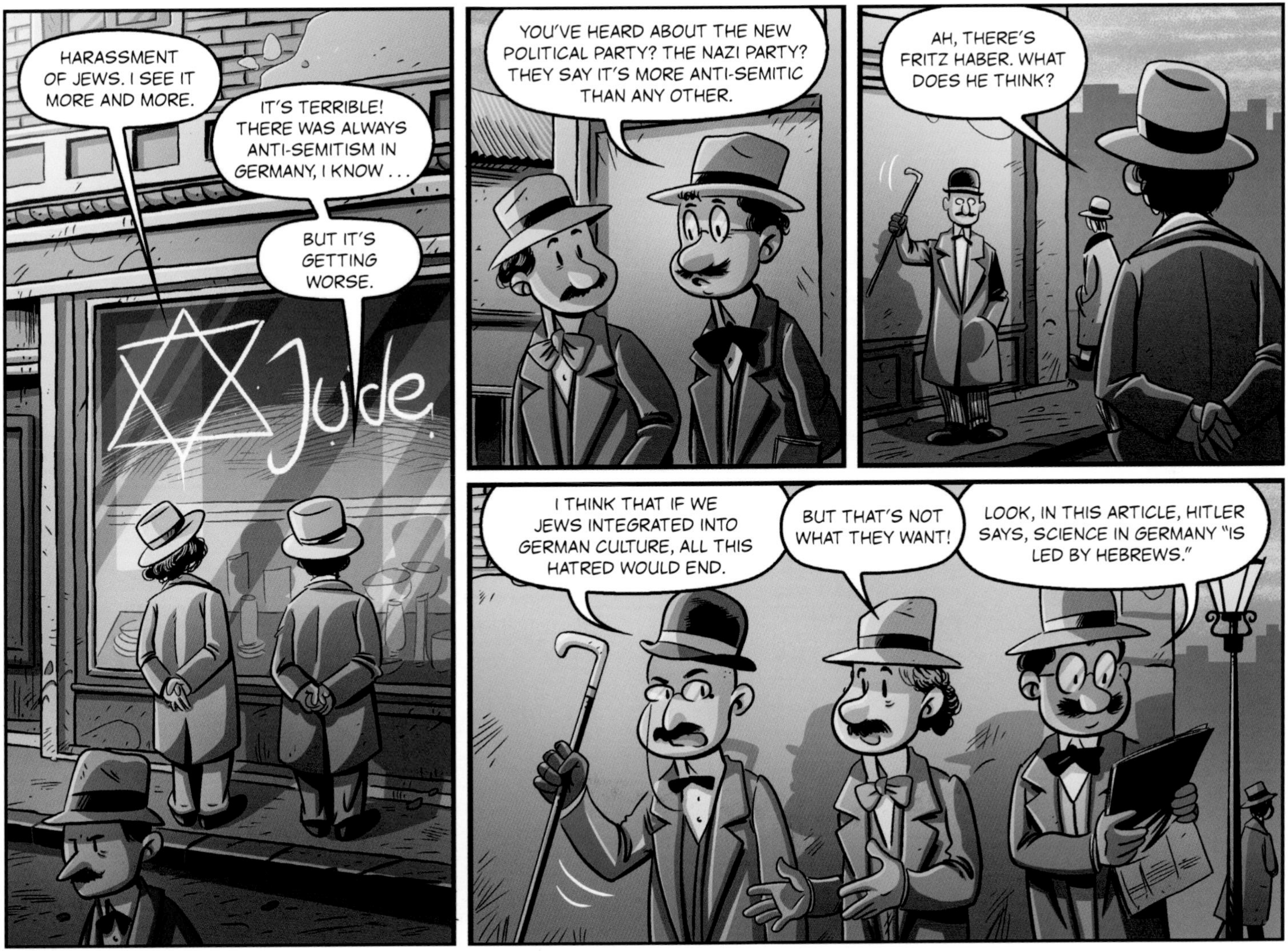
HARASSMENT OF JEWS. I SEE IT MORE AND MORE.
IT'S TERRIBLE! THERE WAS ALWAYS ANTI-SEMITISM IN GERMANY, I KNOW . . .
BUT IT'S GETTING WORSE.
Jude
YOU'VE HEARD ABOUT THE NEW POLITICAL PARTY? THE NAZI PARTY? THEY SAY IT'S MORE ANTI-SEMITIC THAN ANY OTHER.
AH, THERE'S FRITZ HABER. WHAT DOES HE THINK?
I THINK THAT IF WE JEWS INTEGRATED INTO GERMAN CULTURE, ALL THIS HATRED WOULD END.
BUT THAT'S NOT WHAT THEY WANT!
LOOK, IN THIS ARTICLE, HITLER SAYS, SCIENCE IN GERMANY "IS LED BY HEBREWS."

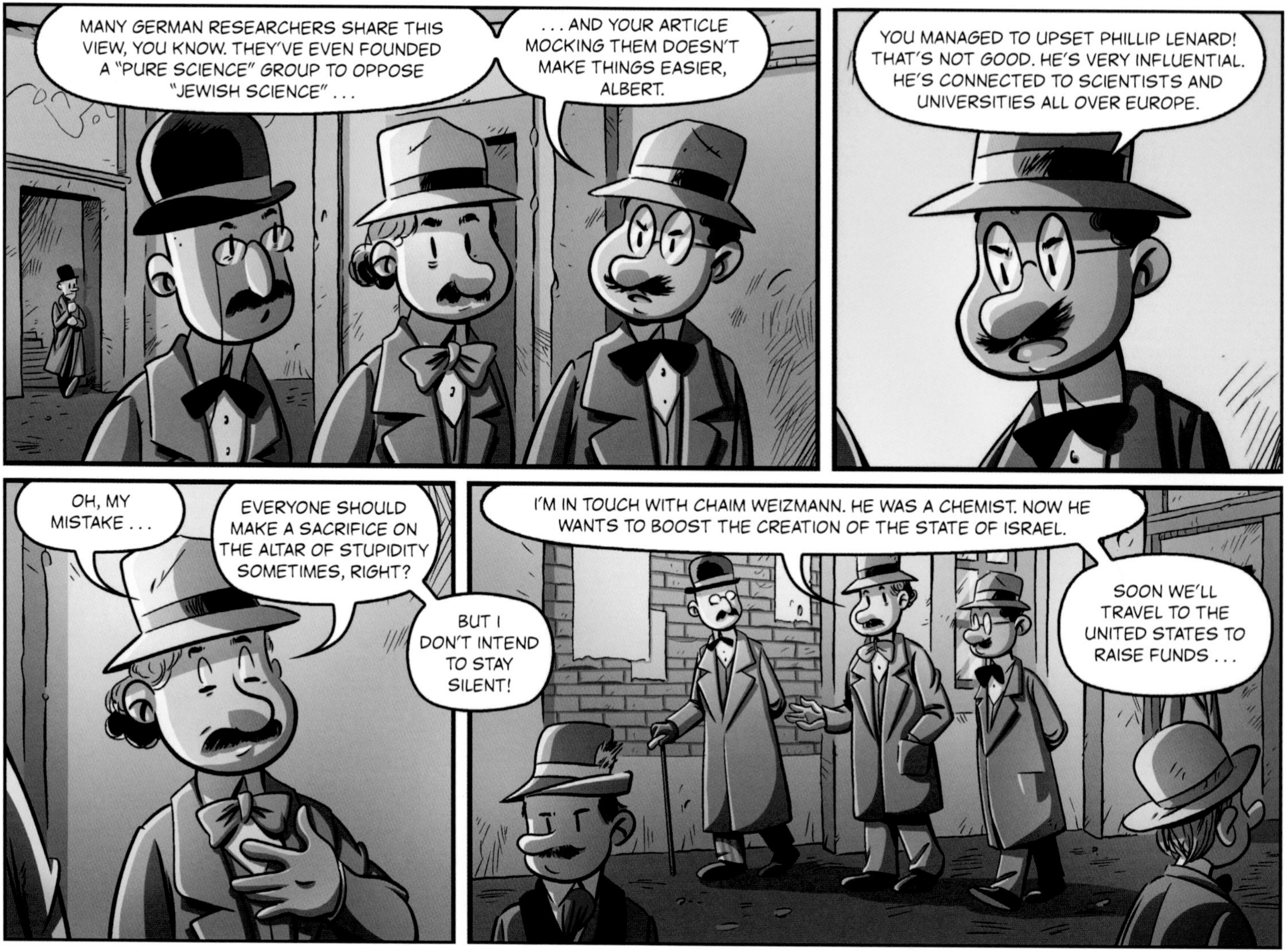
MANY GERMAN RESEARCHERS SHARE THIS VIEW, YOU KNOW. THEY'VE EVEN FOUNDED A "PURE SCIENCE" GROUP TO OPPOSE "JEWISH SCIENCE" . . .
. . . AND YOUR ARTICLE MOCKING THEM DOESN'T MAKE THINGS EASIER, ALBERT.
YOU MANAGED TO UPSET PHILLIP LENARD! THAT'S NOT GOOD. HE'S VERY INFLUENTIAL. HE'S CONNECTED TO SCIENTISTS AND UNIVERSITIES ALL OVER EUROPE.
OH, MY MISTAKE . . .
EVERYONE SHOULD MAKE A SACRIFICE ON THE ALTAR OF STUPIDITY SOMETIMES, RIGHT?
BUT I DON'T INTEND TO STAY SILENT!
I'M IN TOUCH WITH CHAIM WEIZMANN. HE WAS A CHEMIST. NOW HE WANTS TO BOOST THE CREATION OF THE STATE OF ISRAEL.
SOON WE'LL TRAVEL TO THE UNITED STATES TO RAISE FUNDS . . .

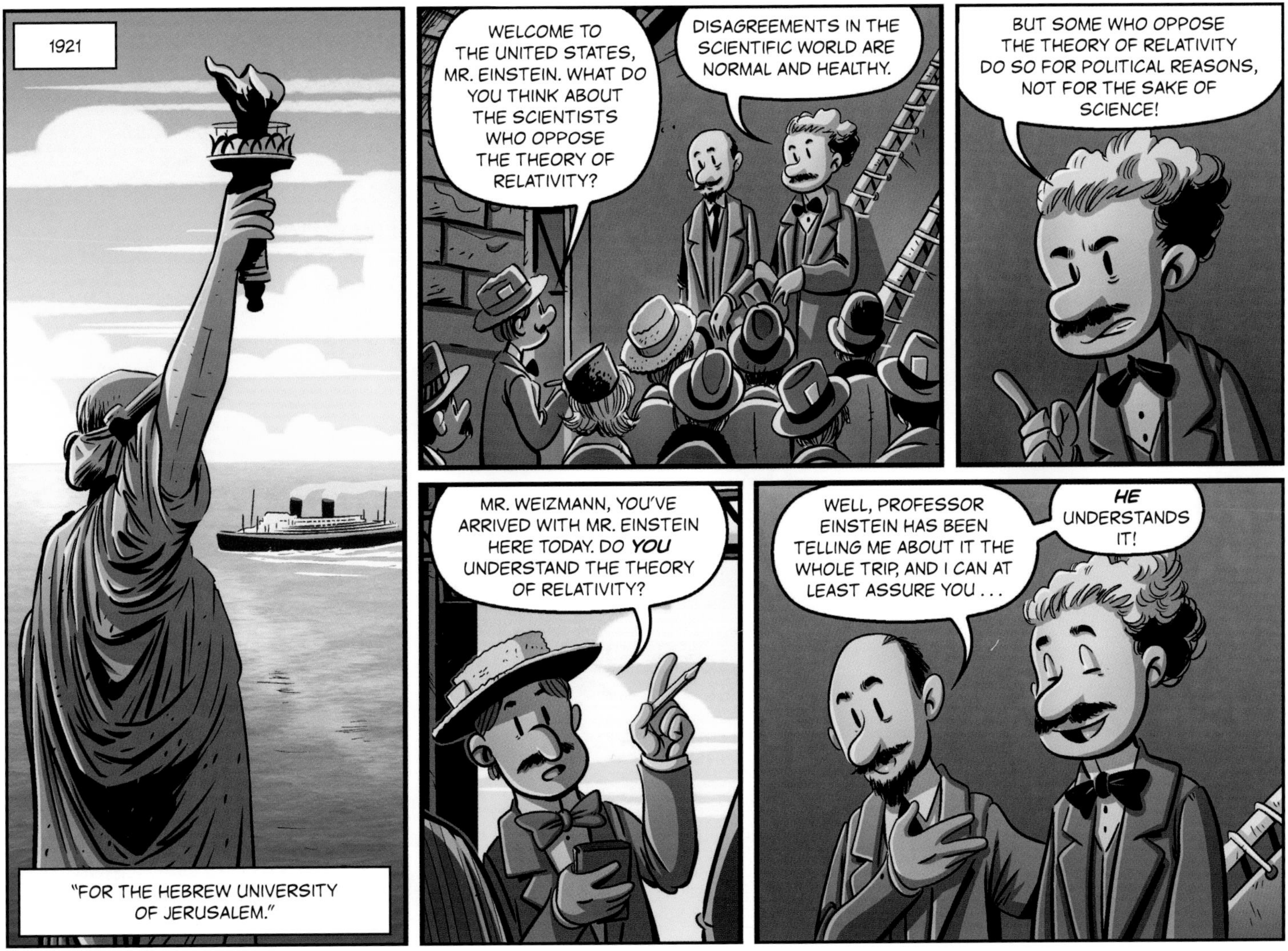
1921
"FOR THE HEBREW UNIVERSITY OF JERUSALEM."
WELCOME TO THE UNITED STATES, MR. EINSTEIN. WHAT DO YOU THINK ABOUT THE SCIENTISTS WHO OPPOSE THE THEORY OF RELATIVITY?
DISAGREEMENTS IN THE SCIENTIFIC WORLD ARE NORMAL AND HEALTHY.
BUT SOME WHO OPPOSE THE THEORY OF RELATIVITY DO SO FOR POLITICAL REASONS, NOT FOR THE SAKE OF SCIENCE!
MR. WEIZMANN, YOU'VE ARRIVED WITH MR. EINSTEIN HERE TODAY. DO *YOU* UNDERSTAND THE THEORY OF RELATIVITY?
WELL, PROFESSOR EINSTEIN HAS BEEN TELLING ME ABOUT IT THE WHOLE TRIP, AND I CAN AT LEAST ASSURE YOU . . .
HE UNDERSTANDS IT!

A CONFERENCE AT
PRINCETON UNIVERSITY

I CAN'T UNDERSTAND ANY OF THIS!

HE'S SPEAKING IN GERMAN . . .

I MEAN THE EQUATIONS.

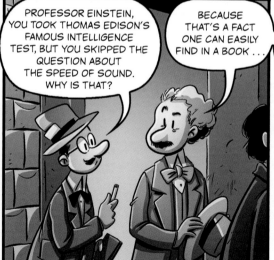

PROFESSOR EINSTEIN, YOU TOOK THOMAS EDISON'S FAMOUS INTELLIGENCE TEST, BUT YOU SKIPPED THE QUESTION ABOUT THE SPEED OF SOUND. WHY IS THAT?

BECAUSE THAT'S A FACT ONE CAN EASILY FIND IN A BOOK . . .

. . . AND THE PURPOSE OF A UNIVERSITY EDUCATION IS NOT TO MEMORIZE FACTS BUT TO TRAIN THE MIND TO *THINK.*

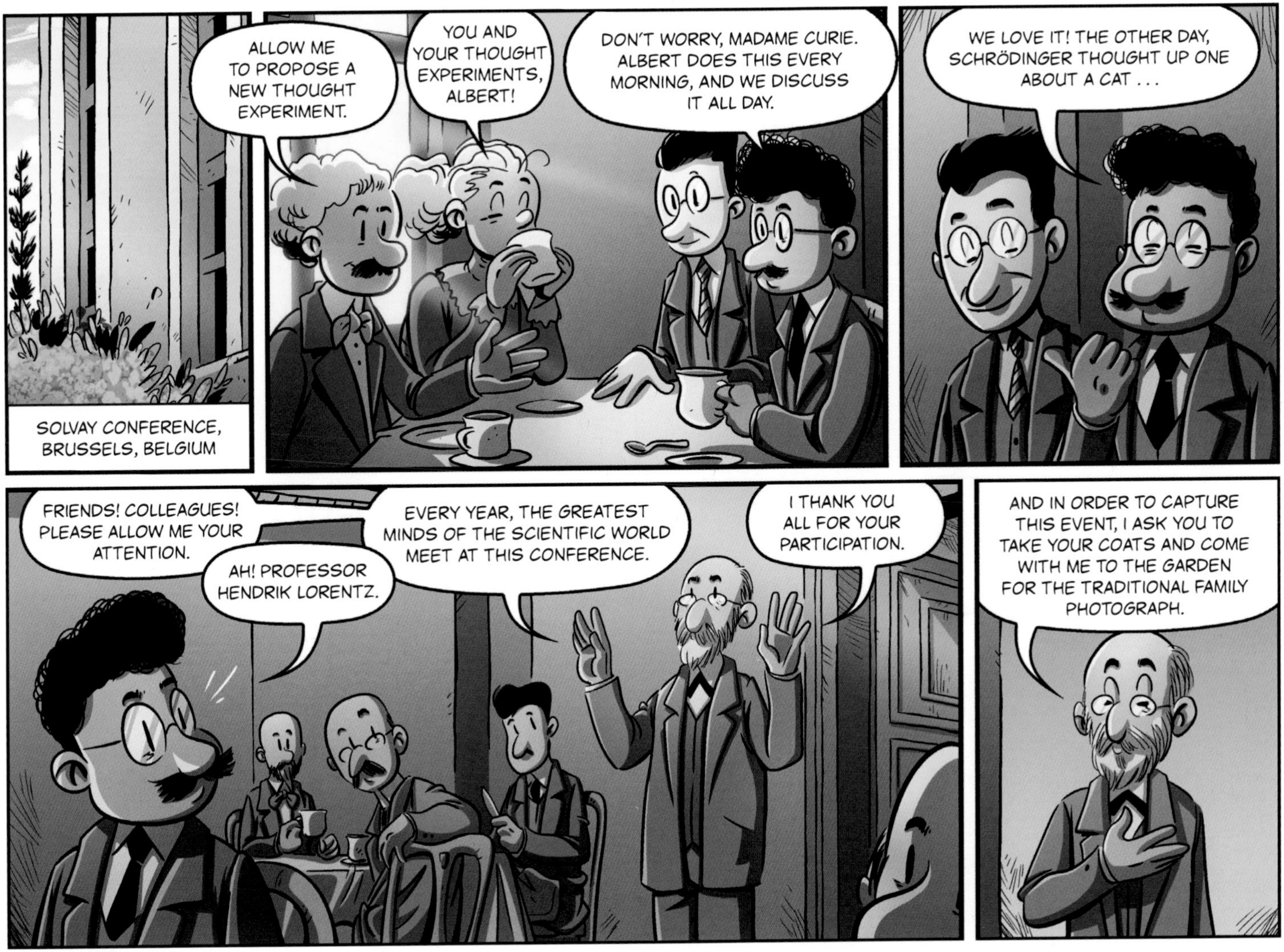
SOLVAY CONFERENCE, BRUSSELS, BELGIUM
ALLOW ME TO PROPOSE A NEW THOUGHT EXPERIMENT.
YOU AND YOUR THOUGHT EXPERIMENTS, ALBERT!
DON'T WORRY, MADAME CURIE. ALBERT DOES THIS EVERY MORNING, AND WE DISCUSS IT ALL DAY.
WE LOVE IT! THE OTHER DAY, SCHRÖDINGER THOUGHT UP ONE ABOUT A CAT . . .
FRIENDS! COLLEAGUES! PLEASE ALLOW ME YOUR ATTENTION.
AH! PROFESSOR HENDRIK LORENTZ.
EVERY YEAR, THE GREATEST MINDS OF THE SCIENTIFIC WORLD MEET AT THIS CONFERENCE.
I THANK YOU ALL FOR YOUR PARTICIPATION.
AND IN ORDER TO CAPTURE THIS EVENT, I ASK YOU TO TAKE YOUR COATS AND COME WITH ME TO THE GARDEN FOR THE TRADITIONAL FAMILY PHOTOGRAPH.

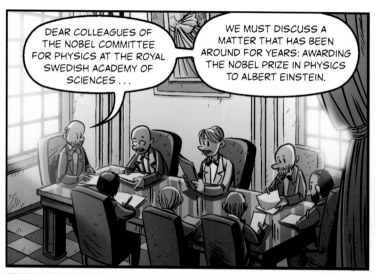

DEAR COLLEAGUES OF THE NOBEL COMMITTEE FOR PHYSICS AT THE ROYAL SWEDISH ACADEMY OF SCIENCES . . .

WE MUST DISCUSS A MATTER THAT HAS BEEN AROUND FOR YEARS: AWARDING THE NOBEL PRIZE IN PHYSICS TO ALBERT EINSTEIN.

TRUE. IF WE DIDN'T GIVE IT TO HIM BEFORE, IT'S BECAUSE AT FIRST HIS THEORIES WERE, WELL . . . TOO THEORETICAL.

YES, BUT NO LONGER. THE 1919 EXPEDITION TO BRAZIL AND THE ISLAND OF PRÍNCIPE MADE MEASUREMENTS THAT THE 1914 PARTY COULDN'T MAKE. THEY SHOWED THAT EINSTEIN WAS RIGHT.

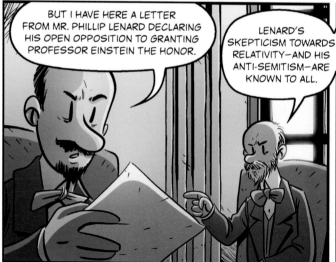

BUT I HAVE HERE A LETTER FROM MR. PHILLIP LENARD DECLARING HIS OPEN OPPOSITION TO GRANTING PROFESSOR EINSTEIN THE HONOR.

LENARD'S SKEPTICISM TOWARDS RELATIVITY—AND HIS ANTI-SEMITISM—ARE KNOWN TO ALL.

BUT EINSTEIN AND HIS WORKS HAVE BECOME SO FAMOUS THAT NO ONE CAN EXPLAIN ANYMORE WHY HE DOESN'T HAVE A NOBEL. BESIDES, SCIENTISTS SUCH AS PLANCK, BOHR, AND HEISENBERG HAVE ALREADY NOMINATED HIM MANY TIMES.

THE TIME HAS COME TO GIVE IT TO HIM. BUT SO THERE'S NO CONTROVERSY, WE'LL AWARD IT FOR HIS STUDIES ON PHOTOELECTRIC EFFECT, NOT FOR RELATIVITY.

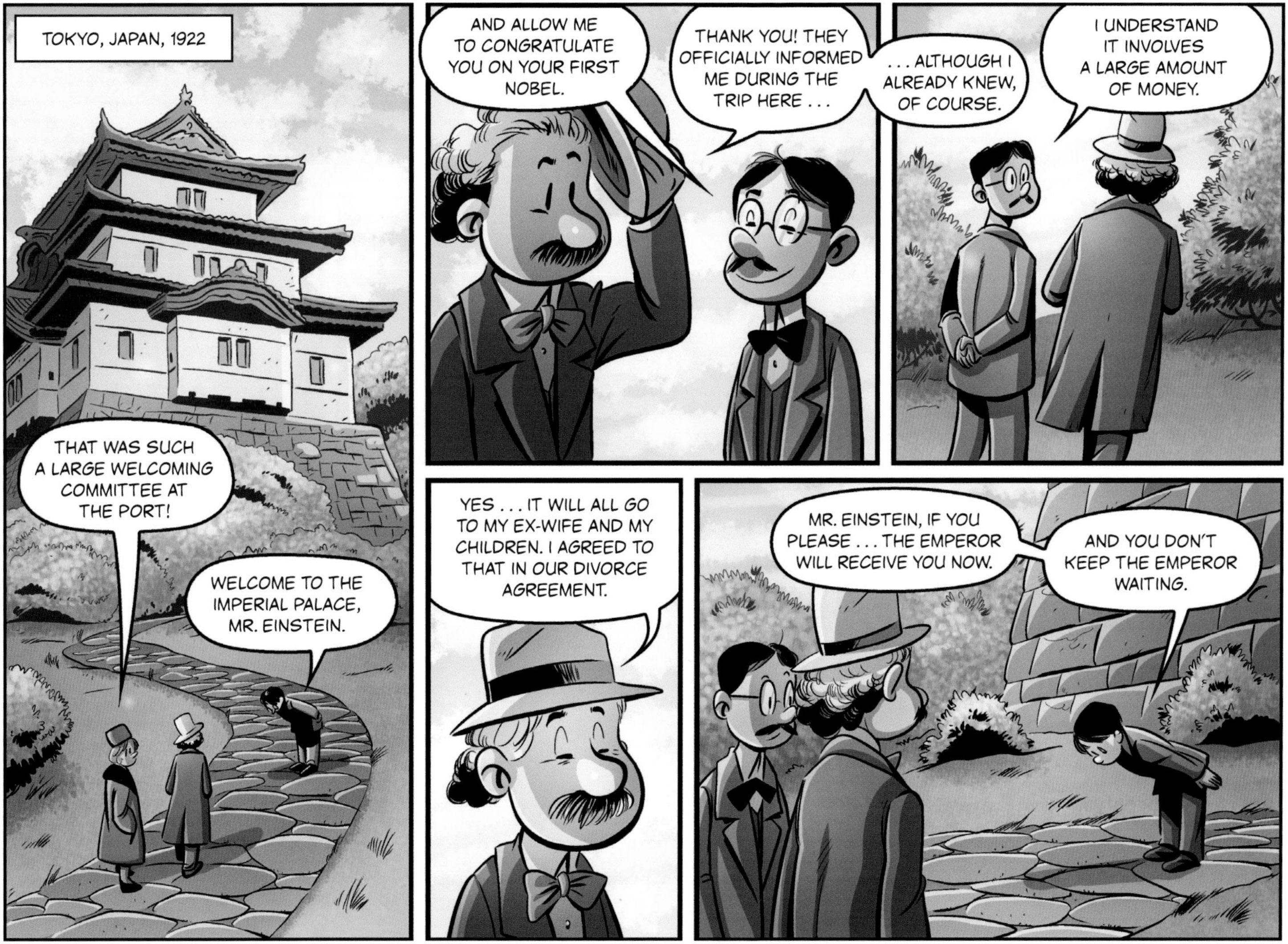
TOKYO, JAPAN, 1922
THAT WAS SUCH A LARGE WELCOMING COMMITTEE AT THE PORT!
WELCOME TO THE IMPERIAL PALACE, MR. EINSTEIN.
AND ALLOW ME TO CONGRATULATE YOU ON YOUR FIRST NOBEL.
THANK YOU! THEY OFFICIALLY INFORMED ME DURING THE TRIP HERE . . .
. . . ALTHOUGH I ALREADY KNEW, OF COURSE.
I UNDERSTAND IT INVOLVES A LARGE AMOUNT OF MONEY.
YES . . . IT WILL ALL GO TO MY EX-WIFE AND MY CHILDREN. I AGREED TO THAT IN OUR DIVORCE AGREEMENT.
MR. EINSTEIN, IF YOU PLEASE . . . THE EMPEROR WILL RECEIVE YOU NOW.
AND YOU DON'T KEEP THE EMPEROR WAITING.

MOUNT WILSON OBSERVATORY, PASADENA, CALIFORNIA, 1931

...THANKS TO THOSE OBSERVATIONS, I COULD VERIFY THAT, IN EFFECT, THE UNIVERSE IS EXPANDING.

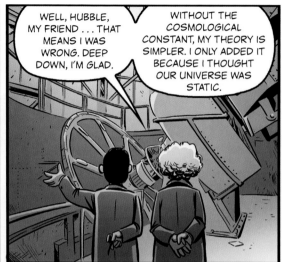

WELL, HUBBLE, MY FRIEND... THAT MEANS I WAS WRONG. DEEP DOWN, I'M GLAD.

WITHOUT THE COSMOLOGICAL CONSTANT, MY THEORY IS SIMPLER. I ONLY ADDED IT BECAUSE I THOUGHT OUR UNIVERSE WAS STATIC.

THAT'S SCIENCE, MY FRIEND. THE OBSERVATIONS OF SOME PROVE OR DISPROVE THE THEORIES OF OTHERS.

WILL YOU RETURN TO GERMANY?

YES... BUT BECAUSE OF HITLER, THINGS THERE ARE COMPLICATED FOR THE JEWISH PEOPLE.

I'M VERY CONCERNED ABOUT THE FUTURE OF MY BIRTHPLACE!

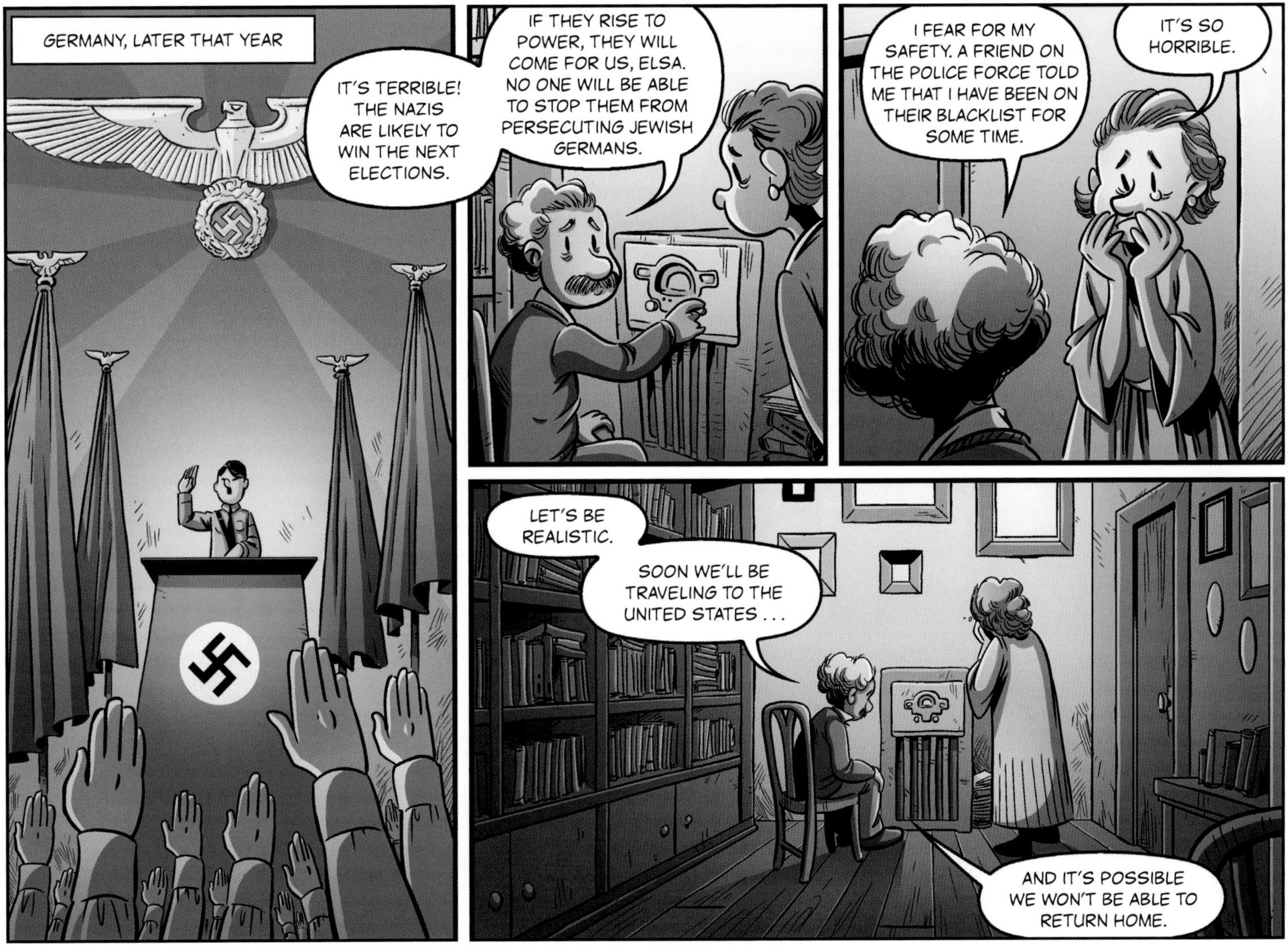
GERMANY, LATER THAT YEAR
IT'S TERRIBLE! THE NAZIS ARE LIKELY TO WIN THE NEXT ELECTIONS.
IF THEY RISE TO POWER, THEY WILL COME FOR US, ELSA. NO ONE WILL BE ABLE TO STOP THEM FROM PERSECUTING JEWISH GERMANS.
I FEAR FOR MY SAFETY. A FRIEND ON THE POLICE FORCE TOLD ME THAT I HAVE BEEN ON THEIR BLACKLIST FOR SOME TIME.
IT'S SO HORRIBLE.
LET'S BE REALISTIC.
SOON WE'LL BE TRAVELING TO THE UNITED STATES . . .
AND IT'S POSSIBLE WE WON'T BE ABLE TO RETURN HOME.

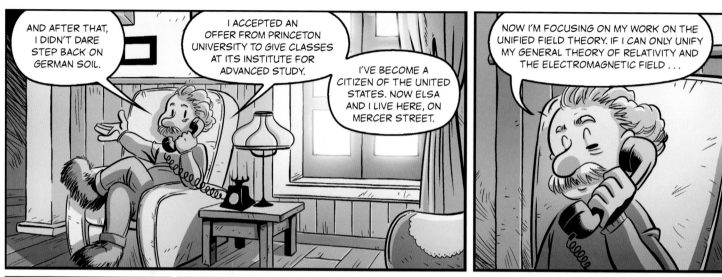

AND AFTER THAT, I DIDN'T DARE STEP BACK ON GERMAN SOIL.

I ACCEPTED AN OFFER FROM PRINCETON UNIVERSITY TO GIVE CLASSES AT ITS INSTITUTE FOR ADVANCED STUDY.

I'VE BECOME A CITIZEN OF THE UNITED STATES. NOW ELSA AND I LIVE HERE, ON MERCER STREET.

NOW I'M FOCUSING ON MY WORK ON THE UNIFIED FIELD THEORY. IF I CAN ONLY UNIFY MY GENERAL THEORY OF RELATIVITY AND THE ELECTROMAGNETIC FIELD . . .

RIIIING

SOMEONE'S AT THE DOOR. I SHOULD GET IT.

OH! HELLO, NEIGHBOR!

HI, MR. EINSTEIN! CAN YOU HELP ME WITH MY HOMEWORK?

IT'S MATH PROBLEMS.

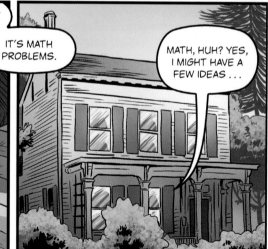

MATH, HUH? YES, I MIGHT HAVE A FEW IDEAS . . .

TIMELINE

1879   Albert Einstein is born in Ulm, a city in the German Empire (modern Germany), on March 14.

1896   He enrolls at the Zürich Polytechnic in Zürich, Switzerland.

1902   He moves to Bern, Switzerland, for a job at the Swiss Patent Office.

1903   He marries Mileva Marić

1905   He publishes the special theory of relativity.

1916   He publishes the general theory of relativity.

1919   He and Mileva Marić-Einstein divorce. He marries Elsa Löwenthal.

1921   He and Chaim Weizmann visit the United States to raise funds for the Hebrew University of Jerusalem.

1922   He receives the 1921 Nobel Prize in Physics.

1940   He joins the Princeton University's Institute for Advanced Study in Princeton, New Jersey. He becomes a United States citizen.

1955   He dies in Princeton on April 18 from complications related to a ruptured aneurysm (weakened artery wall).

GLOSSARY

COSMOLOGICAL CONSTANT: an idea Albert Einstein relied on when he believed the universe was static rather than expanding. In Einstein's equations of the time, the cosmological constant counterbalanced the force of gravity.

FRAME OF REFERENCE: what a person is able to observe from a specific position

GENERAL RELATIVITY: a theory dealing with gravity, including the idea that the force of gravity affects light in addition to affecting objects

GRAVITY: the force that causes objects to fall toward Earth

GYMNASIUM: a centuries-old high school founded in 1607 in Zagreb, Croatia

HEBREW: a descendant of a group of people who lived in Israel and practiced Judaism

INTEGRATE: to combine or become a part of

INVARIANCE: remaining constant across different frames of reference

NOBEL PRIZE: a prize awarded annually for important work in the field of chemistry, economics, literature, medicine, peace, or physics

PATENT: a document that gives a person the sole right to make or sell a certain product

POLYTECHNIC: a college or university that educates students in science and technology

PYTHAGOREAN THEOREM: a mathematical formula that explains the relationship among the three sides of a right triangle

QUANTA: small particles of energy

QUANTUM: relating to very small particles

RADIATION: a powerful form of energy

SERBIA: a country in the southeastern region of central Europe

SPECIAL RELATIVITY: a theory dealing with light and motion, including the idea that light always travels at the same rate but measurements for time and space can change

STATIC: not moving or growing

THEORY: an unproven idea that leads to further study

THOUGHT EXPERIMENT: an experiment performed within the mind and sometimes within conversation

FURTHER RESOURCES

The Albert Einstein Archives
   http://www.albert-einstein.org/

Bayarri, Jordi. *Marie Curie and Radioactivity*. Minneapolis: Graphic Universe, 2020.

Doeden, Matt. *Albert Einstein: Relativity Rock Star*. Minneapolis: Lerner Publications, 2020.

Famous Scientists: Albert Einstein
   https://www.famousscientists.org/albert-einstein

National Geographic Kids: Albert Einstein
   https://kids.nationalgeographic.com/explore/history/albert-einstein/

TEDEd: Einstein's Miracle Year
   https://ed.ted.com/lessons/einstein-s-miracle-year-larry-lagerstrom

INDEX